Victoria Glendinning's

HERTFORDSHIRE

Victoria Glendinning's

HERTFORDSHIRE

with photographs by
Hugo Glendinning

WEIDENFELD AND NICOLSON · LONDON

First published in Great Britain in 1989 by
George Weidenfeld and Nicolson Limited
91 Clapham High Street, London SW4 7TA

British Library Cataloguing in Publication Data
Glendinning, Victoria
    My Hertfordshire.
    1. Hertfordshire. Description & travel
    1. Title
    914.25′804858
    ISBN 0–297–79537–6

Printed in Great Britain by
Butler & Tanner Ltd
Frome and London

For the twins, Frederic and George Seebohm,
who celebrated their eightieth birthday
on 18 January 1989

NOTE: The map provided in this book marks most of the places mentioned, but the essential companion to an exploration of Hertfordshire is the *Hertfordshire Street Atlas* ($3\frac{1}{2}$ miles to an inch) published by the Ordnance Survey and George Philip & Son Ltd. It marks and names not only every town and village street but every country track, path, wood, stream, ruin, ancient site, and every house and farm of any significance.

CONTENTS

	List of Illustrations	viii
	Map of Hertfordshire	x
1	Roots	1
2	Roads	10
3	Consuburbation	26
4	Romans	41
5	Footsteps	54
6	Authors	66
7	Godliness	83
8	Tour	99
9	Houses	116
10	Wen	133
	Notes	151
	Index	155

ILLUSTRATIONS

❧❧

Between pages 52 and 53

The Icknield Way
Pondside Cottages, Graveley
St Etheldreda's, Chesfield
Church Lane, between Gravely and Chesfield
View from Telegraph Hill
View near the sewage works, Hoddesdon
Welwyn Viaduct
The Biggin, Hitchin
Shenley Cage
Georgian Town Hall, Ware
Stevenage New Town
Welwyn Garden City

Between pages 84 and 85

The Eight Bells, Hatfield
Rook's Nest, Stevenage
Orwell's cottage, Wallington
Charles Lamb at Button Snap

Illustrations

Minsden Chapel
Shaw's summerhouse, Ayot St Lawrence
Lombard House, Hertford
Lady Anne Grimston's tomb
St Alban's Cathedral
Disused church, Caldecote
Monument to Sir Hugh Myddelton
Church at Thundridge

Between pages 116 and 117

Brocket Hall, Lemsford
Furneux Pelham Hall
Gorhambury
The Rye House gatehouse
The Old Palace, Hatfield
Hatfield House
Queen Hoo
Temple Bar, Theobald's Park
Barns at Wallington
Pumping station, Chadwell Springs
Cornfield at Caldecote

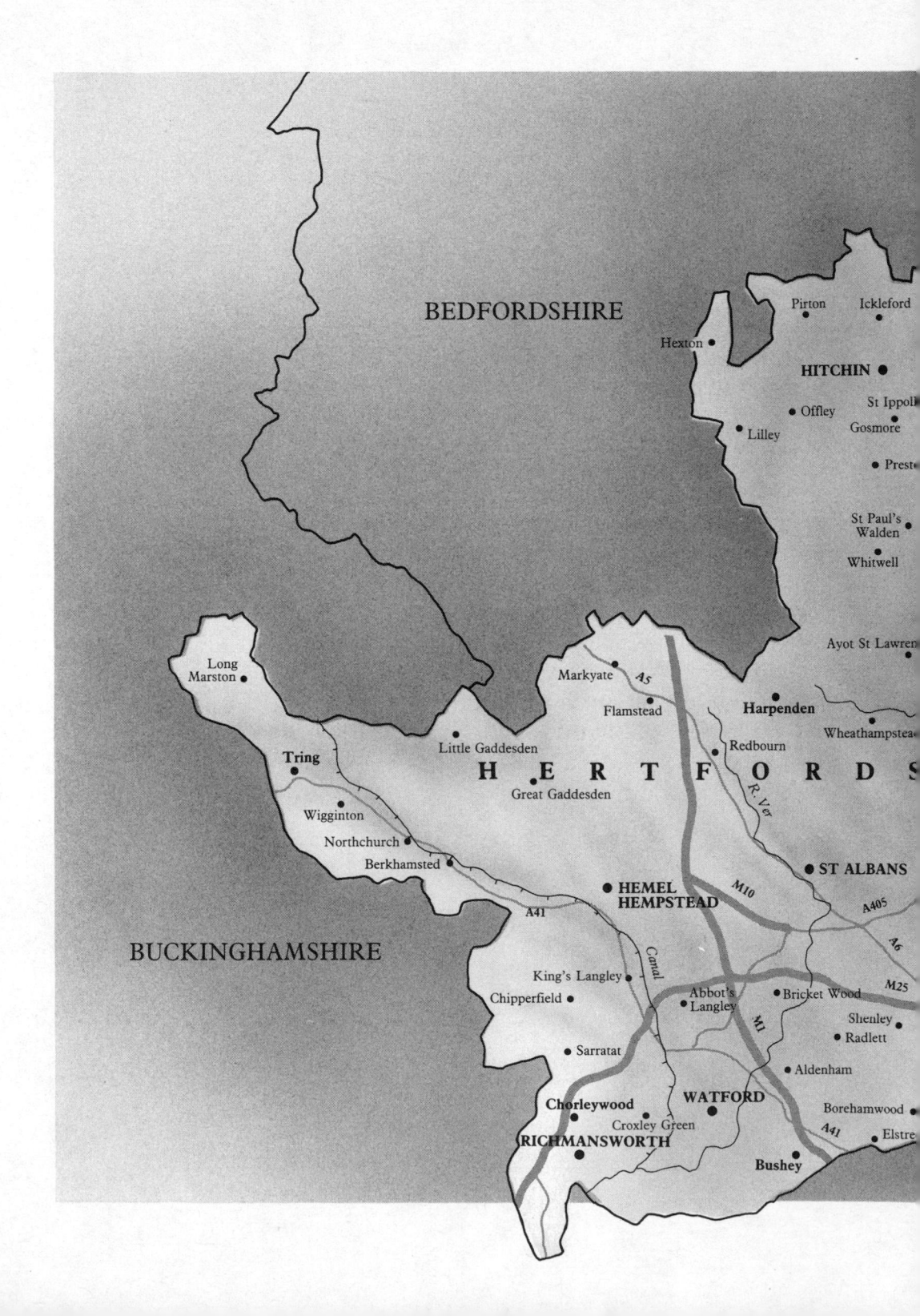

BEDFORDSHIRE

BUCKINGHAMSHIRE

Pirton
Ickleford
Hexton
HITCHIN
Offley
St Ippoll
Lilley
Gosmore
Preste

St Paul's
Walden
Whitwell

Ayot St Lawren

Long
Marston
Markyate
A5
Flamstead
Harpenden
Wheathampstea

Little Gaddesden
Redbourn
Tring
H E R T   F O R D S
Great Gaddesden
R. Ver

Wigginton
Northchurch
ST ALBANS
Berkhamsted
HEMEL
HEMPSTEAD
M10
A405

A41
A6

King's Langley
Canal
M25

Chipperfield
Abbot's
Langley
Bricket Wood

Shenley
M1
Radlett

Sarratat
Aldenham

Chorleywood
WATFORD
Borehamwood

Croxley Green
A41
Elstre

RICHMANSWORTH
Bushey

CAMBRIDGESHIRE

• Hinxworth
Ashwell •
   • **Royston**

• Caldecote
• Newnham   Barley •
Bygrave   • Therfield
   Kelshall •   • Barkway
Radwell   • Reed

• **Baldock**   • Sandon
LETCHWORTH • Wallington
        • Anstey
• Clothall • Rushden
Weston • Throcking •   • Great Hormead
reat   Cottered • Buntingford • Stocking
Vymondeley Cromer • • Hare Street Pelham
• Graveley   • Aspenden • Furneux Pelham
   • Ardeley Westmill •
Walkern • Bassus Cherry Green
   Green   • Braughing
• **STEVENAGE**   • Aldbury
   • Benington Puckeridge • Little
• Aston   Hadham
     Standon •
• Knebworth • Whempstead **BISHOP'S**
   • Watton at Stone **STORTFORD**
Datchworth • Much Hadham •
  Wadesmill •
• Stapleford
Welwyn • Bramfield Widford • Sawbridgeworth •
  Waterford • Thundridge
Digswell • Tewin • **Ware** • Hunsdon
WELWYN
GARDEN CITY **HERTFORD**
H I R E   • Great Amwell

Essendon **Hoddesdon** •
HATFIELD Bayford •
Little Broxbourne •
Berkhamsted
Brookman's Park • Wormley •
  Cuffley • Cheshunt •
South **Potters** • Northaw
Mimms **Bar** Waltham
Ridge   Cross

• **BARNET**

GREATER LONDON

A10 A120 R. Rib R. Ash A414 Canal

ESSEX

0   5 mile
0   5 kms

I should like to thank Emma Thompson for permission to reproduce material from her TV series *Thompson*, John Murray (Publishers) Ltd for permission to reproduce John Betjeman's poem 'Hertfordshire' from *Collected Poems*, and Candida Brazil of Weidenfeld and Nicolson for her editorial skill.

ROOTS

The man thought I said 'Herefordshire'. He was rather deaf. When we had sorted out this misunderstanding, he twisted his face into a grimace and barked contemptuously: 'Hertfordshire? Why would you want to write about Hertfordshire? It's near London!'

That, apparently, was a total disqualification. The nearness to London, in his view, debarred Hertfordshire from any interest whatsoever. It was not 'proper country', not like Devon or Gloucestershire. Hertfordshire, to people like him, is just commuterland, or somewhere you drive through as fast as possible on your way to somewhere else.

Hertfordshire is a Home County. It is my home county. I thought, before I began this book, that I knew Hertfordshire pretty well. I didn't, though I'd had a house here for ten years and had spent time here, on and off, since I was no age at all. But I only really knew my own bit. Though I don't go to church I was 'parochial', locked in my parish, my patch. Beyond this was a circle of territory I knew reasonably well, and various routes and destinations which had become familiar to me over time. Beyond again was another wider circle, and beyond that another, the details getting vaguer and vaguer.

There were many parts of the county where I had never set foot or wheel. Hertfordshire is not large, but there were place-names that I had never even heard spoken. The centre of 'my' Hertfordshire is

Hitchin, in the north of the county. When, during the war, Evelyn Waugh was at Ickleford Manor staying with Randolph Churchill, with his young son Auberon, he 'went for a walk through the depraved quarters of Hitchin'.[1] This is just Waugh's gloomy irony. Twentieth-century Hitchin is anything but depraved. It is on the contrary a comfortable, bustling, rather philistine town, crammed with stout citizens and families from outlying villages stocking up on the substantial necessities of their lives, even if in wartime considerable improvization was needed. Our house is a few miles to the south-east of Hitchin – a cottage in the middle of a row overlooking a pond – one of thousands of Hertfordshire ponds, harbouring as they all do rather more ducks than it can support.

The ducks nest behind the hellebores by our front door, they nest in the hedges between the gardens, they nest everywhere. You see them waddling up the gardens every spring – two drakes to one duck, presumably because paternity is uncertain – doing their househunting. Scores of ducklings are hatched, but few survive. Last Easter Sunday, a brilliant day, the first flotilla of the year struck out on the water – ten or twelve cheeping scraps of yellow, feathery life, which forty-eight hours later had all been snuffed out.

It's not just the predations of cats and rats. It's the fathers, the drakes, who feel threatened by the crowding on the pond and break their children's necks with one swift snap of the beak. This is upsetting for the sentimental spectator, though if all the ducklings survived there would not be room to move on the pond and they would starve anyway. But once we wrote to the Royal Society for the Protection of Birds, describing the annual massacre of the innocents and asking whether something should not be done. We received a dry, realistic reply: 'It is Nature's way.'

People, when they feel threatened by overcrowding, have also been known to react in accordance with Nature's way.

Beyond the pond, my familiar territory is a balloon-shaped area dangling fifteen miles or so south, east and west of Hitchin; northwards, you are in Bedfordshire within a few miles, and I am prejudiced against the flat fields and yellow brick of this part of Bedfordshire.

I have difficulty perceiving spatial relationships. (I'm no good at chess either.) Now, after a year's exploration, I can find my way from anywhere to anywhere in my home county without the map. (I should think so too.) But I still do not see it as a whole. I see in my mind's eye rosaries of villages and constellations of small towns, formed by association or because of the routes I have habitually taken.

Geography is subjective. There is such a thing as emotional distance, as well as physical distance. To someone used to the vast spaces of America, any talk of distance at all in this context is nonsense. New Jersey, where my sister lives, is a small American state and it is about the size of the whole of England. Talking about Hertfordshire, we are talking about a micro-region. But to me Tring, for example, in the extreme and protuberant westward tip of my county, is a foreign place, and should by rights be in Buckinghamshire anyway. Bishop's Stortford and Sawbridgeworth, in what one might call the Far East, seem to me to be filched from Essex. Royston has an air of not being quite sure whether it should not be in Cambridgeshire. As Ronald Blythe writes in his book *Divine Landscapes*, 'If you live in a city, a foreigner comes from another country, if you live in a village, he comes from five miles down the road.'

Ronald Blythe writes also of the parish, not only as a unit of familiar landscape, but as 'the most associative, contentious and distinctive personal region'. Parish boundaries were crucial when the support of the poor depended on them, and parishes, in the past, elicited a football-club sort of loyalty. Vicars and rectors, so peculiarly – to us – prominent in accounts of rural life, were prominent not only because the church was the one social focus for the community but because they usually came from outside the parish.

Blythe takes a lyrical view of the old-time vicar on his rounds, passing on foot or horseback through the lanes, 'taking the same twists as the car takes now, calling out to all the generations who have occupied the farmhouses and planted fields . . . .' His view of the parish as sometimes 'contentious' seems more applicable to my own parish of Graveley when I remember the fourteenth-century rivalry between Graveley and Chesfield. In 1382 John Smith, the parson of Graveley, met Robert Shorthale, the parson of Chesfield, somewhere at the Graveley end of the steep and winding lane that joins the two, and killed him.

Now, five hundred years later, the huge nineteenth-century red-brick vicarage, set back from the lane, is an old people's home, and its successor, the post-Second World War ranch-style vicarage, has become a private house. Graveley, like many country parishes, no longer has its own vicar, but has to share. As for Chesfield, it is one of Hertfordshire's many abandoned villages. Only the old manor house remains, now an equestrian centre, and beside it the ruins of the twelfth-century church of St Etheldreda. This was perhaps already under threat when its parson was prematurely despatched to Heaven; sixty-odd years later, the parishes were amalgamated. Poor, doomed St Etheldreda's has been in disuse since the middle of the eighteenth century. In 1750 the Bishop of Lincoln granted to the few remaining parishioners a licence to demolish the already ruinous church. The materials were used for the repair of Graveley Church, down the hill.

Chesfield Park, nearby, was for the first half of our own century the home of the Poyntz-Stewart family. My Uncle George Seebohm bought the estate after the Second World War and had the old house demolished. This was not the act of vandalism it might have been. The old Chesfield Park was a seventeenth-century brick house with stone architraves but, all local historians seem to agree, 'very little architectural pretension'.[2] It was in an advanced state of disrepair.

Uncle George built on the site a comfortable neo-Georgian house. When his family had grown up and left home and he was already in his seventies, he turned his attention to the ruins of St Etheldreda's, which is on his land. He taught himself how to build in the old local way with flints; on visits to Norfolk he looked in at the priories of Castle Acre and Binham 'and watched the Ministry of Works boys at work, to make sure that I could do it better'. He has worked high up a ladder for weeks and months to save the remaining walls from terminal crumbling. Then he commissioned from Mary Spencer Watson the stone statue of St Etheldreda that now stands beside the old walls.

Uncle George has set a stone in the ground, saying: 'Saint Etheldreda By birth Princess By marriage Queen By choice Abbess 630–649. Her Parish Church for the People of Chesfield Manor Doune Ruinated and Plundered 1750.' I asked him where these resonant phrases came from. He replied: 'So the inscription sounds as though it "came from somewhere". The somewhere was just your old uncle' –

a sort of collage, he said, of pre-1750 words and phrases that had attracted him in local records. Uncle George has been a successful stockbroker; he is also poetical.

He is my father's twin. They, and their elder brother Derrick and younger sister Fidelity, were brought up not far away at the house and farm called Poynders End, just outside the village of Preston. The Seebohms have been connected with Hertfordshire since early in the past century. (As roots go, the roots are relatively shallow.) An evangelical Quaker called Benjamin Seebohm, of Swedish origin, came to England from Germany in 1814. He lived in Bradford, but married Esther Wheeler, a Quaker girl from Hitchin. Their second son was Frederic Seebohm, who read for the bar and was an early commuter, finding it cheaper and more agreeable to live in lodgings in his mother's home town and go up to London by the day. Hitchin was a very quiet place then, in spite of the railway; and between the years 1871 and 1881 its population actually declined.

Frederic married a Hitchin girl, also a Quaker naturally enough – Mary Ann Exton. She was known then as the 'Jewel of Hitchin', though she became a rather petulant invalid as an old woman. Mary Ann's father, William Exton, was a partner in the Hitchin bank of Sharples & Co., which was to be absorbed by Barclays in 1896; today's handsome Barclays Bank in the High Street in Hitchin is the same building where my great-grandfather Frederic too became a partner, and my grandfather Hugh presided as local director before becoming deputy chairman of the board of Barclays Bank Ltd and chairman of Barclays in France.

Great-grandfather Frederic, his Jewel, and their five children lived in the wide and lovely Hitchin street called Bancroft, in a house – or a conglomeration of houses – called The Hermitage. Their garden extended right up to Hitchin Hill. Hermitage Road was constructed when Frederic gave part of his garden to the town, for better access to the railway station. A traveller turning into Hermitage Road in 1902 noticed 'some box trees of so large a size that they set me speculating as to their possible age'.[3] They were all that remained of a garden belonging to Benedictine monks in the fifteenth century.

In the 1830s there were sixty of these already ancient box trees, forming a hedge about 180 feet long. I don't know if there were quite as many as that when my great-grandfather bought this piece of land – it belonged at that time to the local MP – pulled down a dividing wall, and incorporated it into the Hermitage garden.

I have seen an old photograph of the giant box trees when they bordered the new Hermitage Road. They were safeguarded by covenant – the equivalent of a preservation order – but were cut down during the night in 1920. I don't know whether this was semi-official or private barbarism. Shops were built in their place. Frederic also gave the land on which were built the boys' and girls' grammar schools. There is a plaque on the corner of Hermitage Road in memory of 'Frederic Seebohm, Banker and Philanthropist', which I try to salute piously on my way to do the Saturday shopping at Safeway.

Frederic Seebohm was not only a banker and a philanthropist, he was a historian. (The thinking banker seems to be an endangered species these days.) He published books on Sir Thomas More and Erasmus, a textbook called *The Era of the Protestant Revolution*, and in 1883 a book of economic history called *The English Village Community*, which was about land tenure and the open-field, or strip, system of farming which was swept away by enclosure. He believed in using material close to hand, and began this book by stating that the distinctive features of the open-field system could be most easily learned by the study of an example: 'The township of Hitchin, in Hertfordshire, will answer the purpose.' As indeed it did, since Hitchin was still a Royal Manor at the time he was writing, so vestiges of its ancient open-field system remained intact.

Frederic was a rather noble person, and the Quakers have a deservedly fine reputation. The Hitchin Seebohms, with their fellow-Quakers the Extons, Lucases, Tukes, Wheelers and Ransoms, are buried in Hitchin in the old Friends' graveyard behind the modern (1959) Friends' Meeting House, built on stilts, which confronts you as you walk up Brand Street to Paynes Park. But it was not always comfortable, as we shall see, to be a Quaker in Hertfordshire.

Even in my great-grandfather's time some vestiges of social rejection survived. The grandest family of the town in those days were the Delmé-Radcliffes, who lived at Hitchin Priory. The priory had been established by Carmelite friars in the early fourteenth century. A few years after the dissolution of the monasteries under Henry VIII it was picked up by a Radcliffe, and remained in the family ever since; they remodelled it in the eighteenth century. (It is now an adult education college.) The Seebohms, for all their respectability and prosperity, and for all Frederic's scholarship and philanthropy, got invited with everyone else to the large annual garden party at the priory, but were never asked to dinner. It is worth recording – because they minded.

The first book I wrote[4] was about one of Frederic's daughters, my great-aunt Winnie, who died of asthma at the age of twenty-two. Another daughter, Freda, was also a casualty. She went insane. Her sisters Juliet, Hilda and Esther did better. Juliet made a late marriage, and was a very good amateur water-colourist. Everyone in the family has 'Aunt Juliets' hanging on the walls. I have a charming picture by her of a corner of Hitchin market-place, looking down Sun Street, when the square was still full of stalls and booths. (Today it is a car-park.)

When they were old ladies Esther and Hilda, unmarried, lived together in Hitchin in a large Victorian villa on high ground called Little Benslow Hills, which is now a music school, administered by the Benslow Music Trust. I walked up to the house only recently; even though there are utilitarian additions, and brutal stretches of concrete and Tarmacadam all over the drive and front garden, when I looked at the heavy front door and glimpsed the evergreens and the lawn beyond I remembered being taken there as a child – stained glass, a dark dining-room, a formal afternoon tea laid out on a shiny table, and the uncomfortable necessity of behaving very properly.

It was Hugh, the younger brother of Juliet, Freda, Esther and Hilda and the only boy in the family, who built Poynders End, just before the First World War. The architect was Geoffrey Lucas, and it is a severe, rough-cast, vaguely Tudor house with massive brick chimneys and no great beauty – or so it seems to me now, though it had great glamour for me in childhood.

During the early part of the Second World War we – my brother, sister and I – lived at Poynders End for a time when my mother went to be with my father at Newcastle. I remember the smell of the house, which was really the smell of the oak used for the wide staircase and the floor of the big drawing-room. The cook was called Ellen Paternoster – a surprising surname, still not uncommon in these parts.

Hertfordshire has a tradition of colourful names. The local historian Reginald Hine collected examples from the sixteenth and seventeenth centuries: Lamentation Caudle, Greediana Tarboy, Adored Tuffnail, Humiliation Scratcher.[5]

I trespassed in the garden of Poynders End the other day, and peered through the beech and yew hedges to the lawn at the back where, as a child of three or four, I lay on the grass and called to my step-grandmother Mysie at an upper window: 'There's something I've got to learn how to do!'

'I know what it is,' she replied hopefully. 'You've got to learn to read.'

'No,' I said. 'I've got to learn to *whistle.*'

My father's elder brother Derrick inherited Poynders End, but the farm did not pay and it all had to be sold. My father – another Frederic Seebohm – has followed family tradition by going into Barclays Bank, and becoming a vice-chairman and chairman of what was then called Barclays DCO (for Dominions, Colonial and Overseas). He and my mother have owned two houses in Hertfordshire. The first was a weekend cottage with its own electricity generator (very noisy) at Sootfield Green, which is just outside Preston, at the junction of the road to Charlton and the track called Dead Woman's Lane. I used to stay there when my own children were babies. The second was a large pink house in a village called Chapmore End, north of Hertford, a particularly muddy village.

Sootfield Green, Poynders End, Chapmore End ... Hertfordshire is full of 'Greens' and 'Ends', some of them very picturesque-sounding: Babbs Green, Bassus Green, Bericot Green, Bird Green, Bozen Green, Broken Green, Cole Green, Friend's Green, Hay Green, Kettle Green, Labby Green, Letty Green, Mangrove Green, Margery Green, Patchetts Green, Roast Green, Roe Green, Rush Green, Sedge Green, Starlings Green, Tea Green, Wellpond Green. There are several Water Ends and Green Ends – and Barleycroft End, Brook End, Chatter End, Clay End, Dancers End, Dane End, Ford End, Great Revel End, Jockey End, Nup End, Pain's End, Patient End, Reed End, Snow End ... That's enough to be going on with, there are lots more. Mostly, they are as picturesque as their names.

A Green or an End, in Hertfordshire, can be a village, or a small scatter of cottages, a single farm or house, or nothing at all. There's no way of telling until you get there. Though one thinks of the village green as being a central focus, very often it is not. Small settlements, originally made by clearing a space – often triangular – in the original forest, grew up close together. The one that got the church prospered and became the village proper. Ends are just what they sound like – a dwelling or a group of dwellings, or the site of former dwellings, on tracks leading nowhere else originally, as is sometimes still the case.

Many villages have four or five satellite Greens or Ends – Ardeley has Church End, Gardners End, Wood End, Munchers Green, Moore Green, Parkers Green, Wateringplace Green – though some Greens and Ends have no village with which they seem to be associated. Some Greens are just grassy tufts at a crossroads, some are so wide as to be more properly called a common – like Roe Green near Sandon, where the road bisects such generous stretches of grass that the cottages recede into the middle distance.

Thirty or twenty or even fifteen miles from London, there are small communities that a stranger would never find, and an atmosphere of silent remoteness. 'Communities' is too cosy a word for some of these places. The sense of withdrawal is overwhelmingly strong, for example, at Bassus Green, which is a featureless loop in a lane where a few hunched cottages squat in a random fashion, facing one another obliquely like cats in a cellar. On an overcast day the cloud presses down on Bassus Green and turns the trees and hedges to pewter. This is an old, residual remoteness. The large and lively village of Walkern is only a mile away. But Bassus Green, mute and wary and almost non-existent, remains a tentative clearing in a forest that is no longer there. A short track leads to Walkern Bury Farm, where there are ancient earthworks – a ring and bailey – and a bit of moat. Not enough has happened here since those fortifications collapsed to clear the sullen hostility which may have made them necessary.

2

ROADS

All day and all night the juggernauts, the long-distance coaches, the executive saloons, tradesmen's vans and family hatchbacks roar north and south to and from London through Hertfordshire on the motorways – the M1 to Birmingham, the A1(M) to York and Scotland. There's a quick burst of something called the M10, running into the M1 from the east; and a long segment of London's orbital motorway, the M25.

From the motorways, Hertfordshire is meaningless. Its mildly sloping fields and woods could be anywhere. You see no towns or villages except, from the A1(M), Stevenage New Town off to the east. To me it looks like a big pity, but one modern commentator has written that 'perhaps the only beautiful scene from a motorway is of the lights of Stevenage seen from the south on a clear night'.[1] Maybe he was not being ironic; we too are pleased to see the lights of Stevenage if only because it means we are nearly home.

The same writer has an inspired appreciation of the giant electricity pylons, the Eiffel towers that straddle the fields near us, linked by multiple cables as if they were holding hands with outstretched arms. He altered my perception of these overwhelmingly tall (and probably health-endangering) structures by his image of them 'leaving their nests like H. G. Wells's Martian invaders', marching from Little Wymondley to Stocking Pelham with 'a Regency grace'.

But there is something sinister about the Martians' nests. Stocking Pelham is a quiet and remote village on the border with Essex. The transforming station, with its huddle of squat structures from which the pylons start their march, looks ugly and threatening. A footpath signposted from the village 'To Crabb's Green' seems to lead right into the heart of the nastiness, as indeed it does; Crabb's Green Farm is just outside the perimeter fence.

There is nothing new about the unceasing flow of traffic through Hertfordshire. Roads have been fanning out northwards ever since the settlement on the banks of the Thames, which is now London, was established. The roads built by the Romans for the most part followed ancient tracks. There were far more of these tracks than were ever made into roads, and most of them are still there.

The Romans transformed the tracks into hard roads made from four layers of stone consolidated by ramming, and up to three feet deep. The top layer was a pavement of blocks of fine stone carefully joined – though in barbaric Britain they sometimes made do with a surface of cobbles or hard gravel. In Hertfordshire they probably used flints set in mortar. The paved part was about fourteen feet wide, with unpaved paths on each side, half the width of the road again. The Romans marked their roads with milestones, and put up *mansiones* – sort of inns, for travellers – along the way.[2] It is no exaggeration to say that after the Roman legions left Britain in the early fifth century, Hertfordshire roads did nothing but deteriorate until the 1900s. Saxton's 1577 map of Hertfordshire, like other county maps of the period, is conscientious about towns, villages, rivers, woods, hills and great houses, but does not mark a single road.

But the great Roman roads that ran through Hertfordshire were never wholly abandoned. The road to Cambridge, now the A10 and formerly the Old North Road, is in part the Roman Ermine Street from London to York. The Roman Watling Street went through St Albans on its way to Chester, and is now the A5183. Akeman Street ran through what is now Bushey and Watford, through Hemel Hempstead, Berkhamsted and Tring, and is now the A41.

There is astonishing continuity; but a road is never definitive. In the ten years we have been in Hertfordshire, the A1 has been almost continuously under modification. The latest improvement is the Hatfield Tunnel, which cuts out a couple of roundabouts and the car radio, usually at the part of the programme I particularly want to hear. The tunnel shortens the journey home by ten minutes, but deprives the traveller of a sight of the Comet Hotel, complete with Comet on the forecourt, for years a key landmark.

In the Dark Ages the great Roman roads became half-obliterated by earth and grass. Some stretches were lost altogether. Others survive as tracks, reverting to their pre-Roman condition. There is a long walk that you can discover only by looking at the map, and seeing its trajectory there, as you cannot on the ground. A minor Roman road survives as the A507 for a few miles out of Baldock towards Buntingford; near Clothall this old route diverges from the metalled road and continues as a track called Back Lane – one of several Back Lanes in these parts – which runs across country to Hare Street, between Ardeley and Cottered.

Hare Street is not a street at all, but two extremely old farmhouses at a crossroads, one of them with a square brick dovecote, crawling with white doves. Just to make things difficult, there is a village called Hare Street about three miles to the east, on the other side of Buntingford. Half a mile south of this second Hare Street you come to a village called Hay Street. You need not worry about any of this. But it makes map-reading in this patch of the county a little surreal, for strangers.

Back Lane, which we abandoned for a moment at the first Hare Street, carries on through the fields in a dead straight line south-east till it peters out near Cherry Green. It's about ten miles from Clothall – a perfect day's walk. In the medieval period the word 'journey' retained its literal meaning – a distance that could be covered in a single day. Our phrase 'a day's journey' is, strictly, tautology.

Medieval pilgrims to St Albans, on the other hand, enjoyed all the excitement of a touring holiday. The major fairs, where everything for the coming year was bought and sold, labourers were hired, and people from isolated villages had the chance to see new faces and meet someone to marry, were huge events; in the preceding days, the lonely roads were humming with travellers, pedlars, entertainers, flocks and herds of animals, loaded carts. Since there were no signposts, and most journeys were cross-country – over heaths and commons, through woods, along unmarked tracks – travellers from a distance often needed local guides between the towns. (Even as late as the early nineteenth century, someone like William Cobbett, an inveterate traveller, sometimes needed a guide on his Rural Rides.)

The social mobility of the seventeenth century brought greater geographical mobility. The Great North Road, which was the A1 before the route was partially changed by its transformation into a motorway, only became important at this time, though parts of its Hertfordshire stretch are Roman.[3] Our A1 sometimes overlays, sometimes crosses, and sometimes diverges from the former Great North Road.

Stage-coaches were struggling north and south along the potholed Hertfordshire roads by the mid-century. In the 1680s the coach took five days to reach London from York; the last night's halt was at Stevenage. The stage-coaches shared the roads with carriers' carts, official messengers, and stage-waggons – which were the poor man's stage-coaches and proceeded at a lumbering two miles an hour. Pepys the diarist, who was perpetually travelling across Hertfordshire to visit his family in Huntingdonshire, found the roads appalling, even in the vicinity of the capital; the way between Finchley and Barnet was 'torn, plowed and digged up'. One of the worst was the Old North Road which passed through Hoddesdon and Ware to Royston. Between Ware and Puckeridge, travellers sometimes drowned in the floods.

With the increasing traffic, something clearly had to be done. Towards the end of the seventeenth century the toll system was initiated, later to be administered by local turnpike trusts, the proceeds going towards the improvement and upkeep of the roads. Hertfordshire, where the traffic was particularly heavy, had very early tolls. Cobbett disliked the toll roads, and avoided them by turning into the fields, the way some drivers nowadays might go to devious lengths to avoid the motorway. People resented parting with money; cunning travellers whipped up their horses and dashed past the collectors to avoid paying. So in 1695 legislation was passed to permit the blocking of the way with a turnpike, which was a barrier of pikes (wooden poles with sharp steel points) on a pivot. The earliest turnpike in

Hertfordshire was established on the site of the first tollgate in England at Wadesmill, north of Ware on the Old North Road. In the next century the pikes were replaced by ordinary gates; and milestones and signposts, for the first time since the Romans left, came in with the tollgates.

My own village of Graveley is on what used to be the Great North Road, and the George and Dragon catered for the passing carriage trade. Daniel Defoe, passing this way between Baldock and Stevenage in 1725, noted that the road was still so bad – the turnpike trust not yet being in business – that the coaches turned off it and bumped through the fields. So the clever inhabitants of Graveley put up gates across the fields and demanded 'voluntary toll', which people paid rather than go back onto the frightful road.[4] There is a steepish slope down Jack's Hill into a dip at Graveley; before the improvements financed by the trust, it was often impassable. In our own century, it was clogged not with mud but with heavy lorries, until the A1(M) motorway was built, bypassing the village; this stretch of the Great North Road is now mercifully demoted to B197.

South of Stevenage, where the former Great North Road, or B197, runs to Knebworth and Welwyn, it has not been allowed to relapse into tranquillity. As far as the old Roebuck Inn at the junction with the Hertford road, it is lined on both sides by superstores of the hangar variety, trimmed in primary colours.

A famous landmark for travellers on this stretch of road was the Six Hills. 'Upon my right,' wrote Herbert W. Tompkins, walking south in 1902, 'on the very edge of one of the most famous coaching roads in old England, six large, grass-grown mounds stand side by side.' These green mounds or barrows have been variously claimed as the work of the Devil, the ancient Britons, the Romans, and the Danes. Archaeologists have found nothing inside them, but they have always been there. Now, sandwiched between the B197 and the railway, encircled by ring roads, overshadowed by an office building and the Royal Mail sorting office, they have lost their magic – they are grassy pimples, which might have been thrown up yesterday by a manic corporation gardener.

The county is rich in such barrows and pre-Roman burial mounds, especially around Baldock and Royston. And in Royston, near where two old British tracks crossed, there is an astonishing beehive-shaped cave, unique in Britain. It was uncovered in 1742, when workmen improving the pitch used by women selling butter came across a large millstone under the road surface. Under the stone was a shaft, leading to the cave. It was half-filled with debris, of which a hundred cartloads were carried away.

The entrance to the Royston cave is in an alley that leads off Melbourn Street. In 1790 a builder whose premises were down this alley set his men to dig a passageway into the cave, which is the way one enters it today. The bell-shaped interior is thirty feet high; the soapy-looking chalk surface is carved all over with shallow reliefs of saints and Christian symbols (and eighteenth- and nineteenth-century graffiti) which were once painted in colours. It is thought these were done for the Knights Templars, based in Baldock, during the Crusader era; but the cave itself might be much older, and was possibly used as a refuge by the ancient Britons during the Roman invasion. No one is quite sure. The temperature in the cave is a constant fifty degrees, all the year round. The alley that leads to the cave entrance is between an estate agent's and a video hire shop – just another surreal juxtaposition typical of modern Hertfordshire.

Unsprung coaches and carts were sufficiently uncomfortable on the deeply rutted Hertfordshire roads. The traveller on horseback also had the weather to contend with. John Wesley, the eighteenth-century itinerant preacher and founder of Methodism, described a day's ride: 'The wind was turned full north, and blew so exceedingly hard and keen that when we came to Hatfield, neither my companions nor I had much use of our hands and feet. In Baldock field the storm began in earnest. The large hail drove so vehemently that we could not see nor hardly breathe.' He was indefatigable, but Hertfordshire congregations could prove disappointing. At the age of seventy-five, after an arduous journey, 'I preached at noon to fifty or sixty dull creatures at poor, desolate Hertford; and they heard with something like seriousness.'

The mail-coaches, which also carried passengers, were the speediest vehicles on the road; they went at six miles an hour. Coaching was at its peak in the early nineteenth century, when Thomas Telford and John Loudon McAdam were restoring Hertfordshire roads to an almost Roman state of excellence, following not dissimilar methods and principles. The great roadmaker McAdam grasped the importance of drainage for achieving stability. Ten inches of hard material was enough for the traffic of his time; sometimes he left a surface of broken stone, which became a unified surface under the pressure of wheels and impacted mud, but chips and gravel were found to achieve a smoother finish. McAdam was a Scot by birth, but lived in Hertfordshire – right on the Old North Road at Montagu House, 68 High Street, Hoddesdon – from 1826 until his death ten years later. There is a plaque to him in Broxbourne Church.

On these new, dry, smooth roads, the mail-coaches used to race one another; there was a famous collision in the narrow main street of Redbourn (which was a coaching stop on old Watling Street – and still a traffic hazard today, in spite of a bypass) between the Chester Mail and the Holyhead Mail, in which one passenger was killed and lots injured. Day excursions from London into Hertfordshire became feasible; the young men drove out to see the illicit prizefighting or cockfighting at Wadesmill or on Royston Heath, bringing new custom to village inns as well as to the coaching inns which catered for long-distance travellers.

Many coaching inns are still in business today, the wide archways, or 'gazunders', into which the coaches turned either blocked up or still there, leading to courtyards, car-parks or gardens. They are too many to list but the George and Dragon in Baldock, the Sun in Hitchin, the Peahen in St Albans, the White Hart in Welwyn and in Old Stevenage, the King's Arms in Berkhamsted, and the Bull in Redbourn are just a few. Thomas Pickford, founder of the famous removals firm, who died in 1811, was a Hertfordshire man; he came from Flamstead, near Markyate where there is a road named after him.

It's hard not to be romantic about coaching days. But it's best to forget sentimental prints of the sort that are reproduced on table-mats. Travel by coach was never less than arduous, tiring, slow, and uncomfortable. Nor did the roads that had not been macadamized go out of use. The long-distance drovers, bringing sheep and cattle from the north of England to market in London, kept alive the zigzagging network of tracks.

The coming of the railways coincided with the heyday of the horse-drawn traffic, and killed it, putting hundreds of inns (and horses) out of business. Some coaching inns became private houses, others were neglected, half-staffed, unprofitable and run-down. The mails were given to the railways in 1841 (and in 1988 taken away again), and stage-coaches were withdrawn at about the same time. Trains from Euston, King's Cross, St Pancras, Liverpool Street and Baker Street, stopping everywhere, fanned out into Hertfordshire on their way north in the way that the roads did; and there were by the 1860s about ten smaller east west lines.

The railways occasioned Hertfordshire's grandest piece of civil engineering – the Welwyn Viaduct, over the valley of the Mimram river, where Blondin practised for his tightrope crossing of the Niagara Falls in 1862. The viaduct, which at its highest point is a hundred feet above the river, was completed in 1850, and the *Illustrated London News* printed a picture of the first train crossing it. It's built of dark brick, and I admire it. The B1000 runs under one of its arches; Digswell Lake and the heavily half-timbered village of Digswell lie in its lee.

McAdam acknowledged that the coming of the railways was his Waterloo. The main streets of most towns were paved or cobbled; but by the middle of the nineteenth century the smart new 'macadamed' roads that linked the towns were becoming overlaid by earth and grass yet again, used only by carriers' carts and farm waggons. The tollgates were not busy, though some continued in operation into the 1890s, largely as a way of providing occupation for pensioners. John Edwin Cussans, a Victorian historian of Hertfordshire, kept a blue ticket issued to him (price 6d) at the Sacombe gate on the Watton turnpike on 9 July 1875, realizing that 'a Turnpike ticket will in a few years be a curiosity'. This particular road was dis-turnpiked four months later.[5]

Charles Dickens found Stevenage High Street, which with its busy, profitable inns had been such a key stopping-place on the Great North Road in the coaching days, 'wide for its height, silent for its size, and drowsy in the dullest degree'. Only a generation earlier, before the railways, the coaches to York, Berwick, Penrith, Scarborough, Whitby and Hartlepool had all passed through Stevenage, and stopped overnight, changing horses, enlivening the High Street with bustle and clutter and making the citizens prosperous.

The railways, slicing through the fields and bringing noise and smoke, were greeted by many with as much hostility as a traffic-bearing road in a rural area is today. But the truth is that Hertfordshire was idyllic in an undynamic, undemanding way after the railways came, with sleepy silence in the streets of its towns and villages, and in the lanes nothing but birdsong and the wind in the trees. I would like to have been there.

The idyll did not go unobserved. Students and serious young persons in the capital discovered the pleasures of hiking and of the 'walking holiday' in the 1850s and 1860s, and explored the network of lanes and footpaths that crisscrossed Hertfordshire – as they still do. The ancient paths and rights of way that skirt the fields between hamlets and villages are well signposted.

We nearly had an accident recently in the steep lanes leading to Wallington when the driver was transfixed by a dedicated 'rambler' wearing special gear – knickerbockers and astonishingly checked long socks. Hertfordshire continues to attract walkers out for a healthy day in the country. One encounters them on the road in couples and in groups, sometimes with serious boots on their feet, rucksacks on their backs, and a rugged enjoyment in their faces more suited to the rigours of Hadrian's Wall than to our undemanding countryside. The field-paths are still sufficiently paradisical, but the metalled lanes of today are not ideal for walking in. Too often, like our rambler, you have to flatten yourself against a bank or leap into a ditch to avoid death.

He would have seemed a familiar figure to Herbert W. Tompkins, one of the more lyrical writers about Hertfordshire in the days when a motor car was still a rare sight. This is what Mr Tompkins wrote about the Hertfordshire lanes in 1902:

> One often hears the praises of Devonshire lanes, and they are worthy to be praised; but you need not travel two hundred miles from town in search of such. In Hertfordshire are quiet winding lanes that stretch mile after mile ... They lead you into valleys unawares; for often the hedges, festooned with honeysuckle or traveller's joy, tower high above your head and only a gate or gap reveals the further prospect ... Some such lanes in Hertfordshire are so narrow that there is but room for one

to tread their path; others are wide enough for the wheels of the harvest cart, which often wends homeward between high hedges which catch the outer straws and keep them pinioned there for many weeks.[6]

Soon after the walkers discovered Hertfordshire, they discovered the bicycle; and members of the new cycle clubs, in bloomers and stout shoes, wobbled out on to roads that were in a condition unmatched for badness since the seventeenth century. The first recorded organized cycle tour in England started from London in 1873 and bumped along the Great North Road through Potters Bar, Welwyn, Stevenage, Baldock, and out of the county to the north. Cycle clubs still make use of Hertfordshire. On the day that we narrowly avoided the checked knee-socks, looking westwards from the high ground on the edge of Wallington into a deep view of fields, farms and copses, we saw a peloton of cyclists creaming along, their machines shimmering in the sun like a shoal of fish, way down in the valley beyond Cat Ditch.

Inns reopened in the early years of this century for tourists such as these. They also spawned a whole new topographical literature, and stimulated local antiquarianism. Those books of county topography and anecdotal history that you can still pick up in second-hand bookshops – with titles such as *Picturesque Hertfordshire, Memorials of Old Hertfordshire* and Herbert W. Tompkins's own *Highways and Byways of Hertfordshire* – were written for the hikers, cyclists, and early motorists.

Just as the railways killed the coaching trade, so the motor car put an end to the rambler's monopoly of the countryside. With the coming of cars, no old roadway would lie unused ever again. Signposts, traffic signs and mileage indicators demystified shadowy turnings. The county's first traffic jam ever – thirty motor cars – was in Hertford in May 1903, where there was a rally of pioneer motorists organized as a public relations exercise. The mayor of Hertford, Sir Kenneth Murchison, was one of the county's first car owners with his Dion-Bouton Voiturette. The speed limit then was twelve miles an hour. Driving his Dion-Bouton at eight miles an hour through Hertford, Sir Kenneth saw an elderly woman begin to cross the road ahead of him: 'When she saw the car coming she let out a wail, clasped her hands together and fell face downwards on the ground. There she remained motionless, apparently resigned to the fate of being crushed to death by the monster that was bearing down on her.'[7]

The first hit-and-run accident ever reported in England happened in Markyate, in the north-west corner of the county near the Bedfordshire border, in 1905. A four-year-old boy was knocked down and killed in the High Street.[8] It made national headlines and Sir Alfred Harmsworth, proprietor of the *Daily Mail,* offered a £100 reward for information. Unfortunately the owner of the killer car turned out to be Harmsworth's own brother, though he had not been in the car at the time; it was being driven by a chauffeur, who was sentenced to six months' hard labour.

George Bernard Shaw lived at Ayot St Lawrence, amid a maze of lanes. When he first came to live there with his wife in 1906, he had a push-bike and a motor cycle. Then he took to motor cars, and hurtled round the lanes in an unsuitably massive Rolls-Royce involving himself in some unfortunate incidents. Shaw had a chauffeur, called Fred Day, but preferred to drive himself.

Hertfordshire has had to get used to traffic. After the First World War the principal roads were tarred to suppress dust; this was the golden age of the steamroller. Even the twisting lanes were given hard surfaces, to accommodate the cars that nosed into every secret corner of the county. Not all of them: often you come to a Y-junction in the lanes where one way continues as a metalled road and the other reverts to a track. Since both branches lead to farms or hamlets, the decision seems arbitrary, and must have been reached according to some long-forgotten feudal power game.

In those few years at the beginning of the century when horses, bicycles and motor cars coexisted on the roads on more or less equal terms, inns and hotels tried to cater for everyone, which led to some confused advertisements, such as 'Stabling for Motor Cars'. The Green Dragon Hotel in Hertford still bears the announcement: 'Accommodation for Motorists and Cyclists. Good Stabling and Motor Pit.'

After the Beeching Report of 1963 the railways were rationalized, and the branch lines closed. Villages and small towns lost their stations. Given the congested state of today's roads, posterity may see the Beeching reforms as a monumental mistake. But many dead railway lines have come alive again as the twentieth century's contribution to Hertfordshire's tracks and paths. Look to your left, for example, when driving between Braughing and Puckeridge. From the bridge over the dismantled railway you see a green track, along which you can walk beside the river Rib for miles.

It is not only the tracks and field-paths that remain the glory of Hertfordshire. The lanes are still magical. W. Branch Johnson, one of the most devoted of modern local historians, has written: 'They were never made, they grew – until today, metalled though they may be, they twist and writhe up and down, round one blind corner after another, nightmares to the motorist and (though few people will agree) the glory of the county.'[9]

Leave the main road almost anywhere – take, as a very modest example, the westward turn off the A1(M) to Ridge and Shenley, seemingly only just clear of London. At once you are in a country lane, going slow to avoid a boy on a horse, with a kestrel hovering overhead. The old life goes on, within a hundred yards of the uncrossable motorway which slices the countryside, separating traditional neighbours and obliterating the relationships between the farms and villages on each side. Or turn west off the A10 at High Cross, to find yourself in an unbelievably narrow lane winding in linked circles through Potters Green, down White Hill to Dane End and on to Whempstead, from where it runs towards Watton-at-Stone through fine, high, wide country.

You constantly find yourself driving along narrow, crooked roads sometimes only six feet across, where two cars cannot pass; there are passing places scooped out of the verges at intervals. It's a miracle there aren't more accidents. But by some freak of providence there is always a passing place in sight as a car rockets towards you round the corner ahead. In wet autumn weather, when the lanes' hard surfaces are buried under a slick and soggy mass of rotting leaves and mud, and the fords in the bottoms are flooded, you sometimes feel that not much has changed around here in two hundred years.

Sometimes the lanes cross open unhedged fields; sometimes they are sunk deep between high banks and hedges, or trees that form archways over the top, dappling the sunlight, like the way from Preston to St Paul's Walden through Hitch Wood. The lanes evolved over centuries, their apparently irrational wiggles determined by the necessity of avoiding crops, private parks, farms, cottage gardens, ponds, copses. They wind down into valleys and over fords, they crisscross one another at baffling intersections and sometimes describe complete circles for reasons that must once have been obvious but are so no longer.

The lanes are Hertfordshire's private life. Those who roar through the county on the motorways and main roads have no idea of their existence.

The tracks are even more private, and the greatest of them all is the Icknield Way. It was there before the Romans came, and though they used it, and called it the Via Icenia, it has never all been paved. My great-grandfather the historian thought it had once stretched all the way from Land's End to the Norfolk coast. It comes into Hertfordshire in the west crossing Akeman Street at Tring, crosses Watling Street at Dunstable (in Bedfordshire), and re-enters Hertfordshire, becoming a boulevard in Letchworth Garden City; then it continues west over the northern side of Hitchin, passes through Baldock to cross Ermine Street at Royston and so out of the county into Cambridgeshire. Thus parts of it are covered by modern roads, following the old route. Parts of it are not.

A most beautiful unspoiled stretch runs out of the Hexton Road above Lilley Hoo, across the top of Telegraph Hill. We walked along that bit of the ancient track on a glittering Saturday afternoon in mid-August, and met no one except two elderly ladies sitting on a fallen tree beside the track and drinking tea peacefully out of a Thermos.

The track divides into wandering ways off and joins itself up again, there are trees bordering it, and scabious and harebells in the grass, and sprinkles of butterflies. On either side the fields of standing corn slope away, banded by shadows, with inexhaustible views of farms and old black barns made from sagging, bulging weatherboards, their shapes sharply outlined in the theatrical sunlight.

It is not fanciful to say that Hertfordshire fields have a special look. This is partly due to the clarity of the light. A clear day here is uncannily brilliant; the light gives everything it strikes the hard-edged intensity of a surrealist painting. There is a great deal of undulating ground, and characteristically mild hills that make perfect arcs, or pure segments of spheres. In late April and early May some of these segments are a solid, glittering, brilliant yellow with the flowers of rape. But there are very few high hills, except where a spur of the Chilterns dominates the landscape along the borders with Bedfordshire and Buckinghamshire, so there is always a great deal of sky. The other noticeable things are the chunks, strips and wedges of woodland marooned in the middle of fields. These are the residue of the forests that once covered everything, and were left there when the land was cleared. Many of the hedges that divide the fields are also woodland remains, with large trees and woodland flora in among them.

The 'Garden of England' is a title claimed by other counties. But Norden in the mid-seventeenth century described Hertfordshire as 'the garden of England for delight', and travellers have often described it as being like a garden. Daniel Defoe, riding over Bushey Heath in the 1720s with two foreign gentlemen, tells how 'they were surprized at the Beauty of this Prospect, and how they look'd at one another, and then again turning their Eyes every way in a kind of Wonder, one of them said to the other, that England was not like other Countrys, but it was all a planted Garden'. You can see what they meant: 'The inclos'd Corn-Fields made one grand Parterre, the thick planted Hedge Rows, like a Wilderness or Labyrinth, divided in Espaliers; the Villages interspers'd ...'[10]

There is nothing mean about Hertfordshire fields. The farmers often leave grassy headlands, and wide paths along the hedges – though perhaps not so wide as in Cobbett's day. He was riding through the corn country between Redbourn and Hemel Hempstead in June 1822, a century after Defoe, and he also saw Hertfordshire as a garden:

> The custom is in this part of Hertfordshire to leave a *border* round the ploughed parts of the fields to bear grass and make hay from, so that, the grass being now made into hay, every corn field has a closely mown grass walk about ten feet wide all round it, between the corn and the hedge. This is most beautiful! The hedges are now full of the shepherd's rose, honeysuckle, and all sorts of wild flowers, so that you are upon a grass walk, with this most beautiful of all flower gardens and shrubberies on your one hand, and with the corn on the other ... Talk of *pleasure-grounds* indeed! What, that man ever invented, can equal these fields in Hertfordshire?[11]

Modern farming methods have diminished the numbers of wild flower species. But in April in the woods around Tewin there are sheets of white wood anemones, and wild cherries in blossom – even though Tewin Wood itself is penetrated by the Ways, Walks, Drives and Closes of 'executive' homes. Hertfordshire's bluebells in May are another of her glories. Wain Wood near Preston (where John Bunyan used to preach), or How Wood in the fields between Graveley and Weston, are scented oceans of intense, unbroken purple-blue under the trees. And in How Wood at least there has never been anyone there but ourselves.

But don't let your dog off the lead in Hertfordshire's woods and fields, unless he is exceptionally staid or well trained. It's not just a question of rabbits, though there are millions of these. In a hollow meadow beside Maydencroft Lane, just out of Gosmore, I've seen scores of rabbits at one time, jumping around together like children in a school playground. In winter, walking up the hill between Graveley and Chesfield, we've seen hares dancing in the snow.

But the hedgerows, woods and fields are stuffed with pheasants and partridges, so fat and complacent that they can hardly lift themselves off the ground. These gamebirds are everywhere, in the corn, in the stubble, in the undergrowth. You turn a bend in the path and there they are, lazily strutting about as if the place belonged to them. They are 'preserved', so that they can be shot. Walking on the margin of woods between Reed and Barkway I have seen them in an enclosure, like hens.

They've always gone in for shooting birds here. When Elizabeth I visited Sir Nicholas Bacon at Gorhambury between a Saturday and Wednesday in May 1577, the party killed over twelve dozen herons, forty-five larks, and quantities of bitterns, shovelers, pheasants, partridges, quails, mallards, teals and curlews. The records evoke a terrifying number of birds falling out of the air, brought down by titled gentlemen. On 23 October 1846 the Prince Consort himself killed 150 Hertfordshire birds, at a rate of one a minute.

A historian in 1902 wrote that 'there are few counties where game is more strictly preserved for shooting than Hertfordshire', which was looked upon as 'the natural sporting ground of those who are obliged to make London their home'. It was 'difficult to find a farm or a covert that is not preserved'.[12] That is still true today.

John Betjeman's father was one of the London businessmen who went shooting in Hertfordshire. Sometimes he took his son, the future poet, with him. Later in life, John Betjeman made scattered references to 'leafy Herts', 'sky-blue Hertfordshire'; and he remembered those shooting expeditions of the early 1920s with a mixture of distaste and nostalgia in a poem called simply 'Hertfordshire':

> I had forgotten Hertfordshire,
> The large unwelcome fields of roots
> Where with my knickerbockered sire
> I trudged in syndicated shoots.
>
> And that unlucky day when I
> Fired by mistake into the ground
> Under a Lionel Edwards sky
> And felt disapprobation round.
>
> The slow drive home by motor-car,
> A heavy Rover Landaulette,
> Through Welwyn, Hatfield, Potters Bar,
> Tweed and cigar smoke, gloom and wet.
>
> 'How many times must I explain
> The way a boy should hold a gun?'
> I recollect my father's pain
> At such a milksop for a son.
>
> And now I see these fields once more
> Clothed, thank the Lord, in summer green,
> Pale corn waves rippling to a shore
> The shadowy cliffs of elm between,
>
> Colour-washed cottages reed-thatched
> And weather-boarded water mills,
> Flint churches, brick and plaster patched,
> On mildly undistinguished hills –

There's more, but that comes in the next chapter.

3

CONSUBURBATION

Picking up Betjeman where I left off:

> Colour-washed cottages reed-thatched
>   And weather-boarded water mills,
> Flint churches, brick and plaster patched,
>   On mildly undistinguished hills –
>
> They still are there. But now the shire
>   Suffers a devastating change,
> Its gentle landscape strung with wire,
>   Old places looking ill and strange.
>
> One can't be sure where London ends,
>   New towns have filled the fields of root
> Where father and his business friends
>   Drove in the Landaulette to shoot;
>
> Tall concrete standards line the lane,
>   Brick boxes glitter in the sun:
> Far more would these have caused him pain
>   Than my mishandling of a gun.

That was written in the late 1950s. At the turn of the century the population of the whole of Hertfordshire's less than seven hundred square miles was around 250,000. By the mid-1970s, it had passed the million mark. A government report on the problems of Greater London published in 1944 suggested ten possible sites for satellite towns to relieve the pressure on the capital. Hertfordshire, in the event, got three of them. The New Town Act was passed the year after the war ended. Stevenage was the first New Town, then Hemel Hempstead, then Hatfield and the new sections of Welwyn Garden City – these last developed in tandem, with a slender band of green still separating the two. De Havillands aircraft factory was a deciding factor in the Hatfield–Welwyn development.

Stevenage New Town is the one I know best. It was planned for sixty thousand people, but has long overshot that figure. Before the New Town came, Stevenage was 'an old and comely village with a fine wide central street and it was surrounded by some of the best farms in the country'.[1]

At one end of the High Street is a triangular piece of grass called the Bowling Green, where Pepys played bowls while waiting for his wife to arrive on the coach. A former coaching inn by the Bowling Green, where Pepys stayed, is now the Register Office where I was married (for the second time). That is by the way.

The New Town adjoins the old, and the ring roads swirl round it. The residential parts of the New Town are divided into large, low, pale red-brick 'neighbourhoods', based on the villages that they devoured, now unrecognizable, apart from Shephall where the green was preserved, as was Victorian Shephallbury, now a school.

The grass verges are wide, the trees are beginning to grow up, and as in all the New Towns there has been a genuine concern to preserve, or even create, green open spaces with lakes. These are sometimes made from exhausted gravel pits. Stevenage New Town centre was one of the first pedestrian precincts in Europe, and thus attracted a lot of attention at the time. Now it looks undistinguished. Architecture of the immediate post-war period has not weathered well and looks cheap and tacky to the 1980s. The best that can be said of New Stevenage, for me, is that it is useful for people in the villages nearby to have a large Marks & Spencer at hand.

The effect of New Stevenage on Old Stevenage was, at first, to depress it. Competition from the big stores in the New Town killed trade. By the mid-1970s there was only one food shop in the whole length of the old High Street; it was third-rate, and it soon folded. Then Waitrose boldly opened a branch of its supermarket chain. It was immediately successful. The Old Town has been rejuvenated.

In the 1980s, there has been a rash of out-of-town supermarket development, on green-field sites. (Going shopping seems to be every-one's prime recreational occupation these days, to judge from the generous provision made.) These Sainsburys and Tescos are immedi-ately recognizable across country by a particular style of building which seems to have become a convention – a central clock tower flanked by low, fan-like tiled roofs. Vaguely vernacular, the effect is of a cross between a Roman villa and an Edwardian stable block. It is an ingratiating, cosy style, but preferable to the 'functional' system-built egg boxes of the 1950s and 1960s. These comprehensively stocked supermarkets, with cash-card banking facilities and enough parking space, are drawing shoppers from the villages away from the New Town shopping centres, stripping these of whatever bustle and glamour they retain. This is something that the planners are currently worrying about.

Apart from an excessive reliance on brick of a particularly hectic red, all the building of the last ten years seems better than the immedi-ately post-war developments. There is some distinguished recent com-mercial architecture in Stevenage, such as the massive glass Confederation Life building on Lytton Way, rooted on its high bank by glassy skirts, or buttresses. (You can see its other side from the train.)

The big supermarket chains do not always build new. Tesco have had fun recently with their take-over of the old Kayser-Bondor factory at the far end of the wide Georgian High Street of Baldock. This factory had an astounding 1930s arcaded façade, like a Hollywood mogul's idea of the Roman town that once flourished just outside Baldock, between the Icknield Way to Royston and the Roman road to Clothall (and where now, for the first time since the Romans, a tide of building is covering the fields again – Barrett Homes, this time).

Tesco preserved the long façade, erecting their new vast shopping hall behind it. Projects like this have wit and sensitivity, everything one would desire the word 'modern' to convey. It is shameful to think of the unhappy tower blocks and hideous domestic 'units' that were being built and approved of in the lifetime of people still active; and it's obliquely flattering to feel that the architecture of the present moment is more worthwhile.

Or maybe it's just that one's eye is attuned to the 'now'. Pevsner's *Hertfordshire*, for example, compiled in the early 1950s and revised in the 1970s describes Stevenage New Town in enthusiastic, even excited terms. To see it at its worst, visit it on a Sunday when the shops are shut, and the gracelessness of the shopping precincts, unmediated by human animation, can be seen for what it is. In my opinion, Hemel Hempstead is the most successful of Hertfordshire's New Towns, perhaps because it seems the most successful commercially, and because the Marlowes centre links up, with an organic naturalness, with the old sloping High Street.

For more than a century, Hertfordshire has been the laboratory for experiments in social engineering, new kinds of town planning and new ways of living, absorbing – not always willingly – the overspill from London. Before Hertfordshire's New Towns came Hertfordshire's Garden Cities. John Betjeman did not like these either. He wrote a derisive poem called 'Group Life: Letchworth'. The early enthusiasts of the Garden Cities, and Letchworth in particular, were associated with sandal-wearing, vegetarianism, folk-dancing, teetotalism, and vaguely left-wing 'new life' idealism. There's nothing wrong with any of that in my opinion, but it is easy to make fun of. For sixty years Letchworth was a temperance town; even now there are not many pubs.

In 1901, there were only 566 people in the parishes of Letchworth, Norton and Willian combined. Norton and Willian survive as villages on the very edge of Letchworth, which grew relatively slowly. Like the New Towns, Garden Cities were designed to relieve London's overcrowding. The dream was Ebenezer Howard's, the author of a book called *Tomorrow* (1898); within four years the Garden City Pioneer Company had been founded with a share capital of only £20,000. By 1919 Letchworth Garden City had 10,000 inhabitants, and by 1961 25,000. The population now stands around 30,000. There's something bizarre about the fact that the Country Gentlemen's Association has its headquarters in Letchworth. (And the Wine Society, another aid to traditional good living, is in New Stevenage. If you collect your order instead of having it delivered, by the way, you get a discount.) Aptly enough, Weidenfeld & Nicolson, the London-based publishers of this book, hold their sales conferences in Letchworth, in the same building where the book is being stored before reaching the bookshops and the reader's hands.

'The most striking thing about Letchworth is that there is nothing striking to see,' wrote one commentator in the mid-1970s.[2] Letchworth is too grand and sprawling a creation to have a village atmosphere, yet lacks the adrenalin of a town, still less of a city. Letchworth is cold. The north-east wind flays the pedestrian who braves its wide, straight boulevards and avenues, though the fully mature trees and gardens – Letchworth was very well planted – must make the place less bleak now than in any other phase of its development. The people who live in Letchworth love it and, like all the Garden Cities, it is proud of its heritage.

In 1919 Ebenezer Howard's company bought part of the Cowpers' Panshanger estate, and a bit of Lord Salisbury's land, and Welwyn Garden City began to take shape. Howard's idea was that people in Garden Cities should find work near their homes, 'in a pure and healthy atmosphere'. It was easier to build houses than to attract businesses and factories. One of Letchworth's earliest factories was Spirella, making ladies' corsets. Apart from the aircraft industry rather later, Welwyn's chief employer was the Welgar Shredded Wheat factory ('Welgar' being a cheery contraction of the full name of its location).

The Garden Cities and New Towns were emphatically not intended as dormitories. But an early-morning look at the rows of cars in the station car-parks of the Garden Cities and New Towns today suggest that in spite of the 'industrial areas', and the chemical, photographic and electronics factories, in spite even of British Aerospace in New Stevenage, a great many people commute to the Wen daily.

In another poem, 'The Town Clerk's View', Betjeman described the sort of England he dreaded as looking 'like Welwyn mixed with Middle West'. Both Welwyn and Letchworth Garden Cities, in fact, have a definite look of small towns in the Middle West of America, or

Canadian prairie towns. Their geometrically planned centres look somehow academic; Welwyn's, with its fountain and cherry trees, is actually called the Campus. Such municipal pompousness is not natural to Hertfordshire. Garden City planners built cottage-style homes, but they thought big. A building that could be an American state capitol is actually the Welwyn Department Store – which used to be called just that, and is now a branch of the John Lewis Partnership and a very welcome one: you can park directly outside it even on a Saturday afternoon. It was completed just before the Second World War.

Hertfordshire seems picked out by fate, and planners (people who have strong ideas about how and where *other* people should live), as terrain for experiment. But it's too easy to blame cranky planners for everything that goes wrong. If there was no planning, there would not by now even be a Green Belt to defend.

You might imagine that George Bernard Shaw, himself a teetotaller and a vegetarian, would be in favour of the Garden City idea. But he was sceptical. In his play *John Bull's Other Island* (1904) he creates a well-meaning if absurd Englishman called Broadbent who dreams of righting the wrongs done by England to Ireland by establishing a Garden City over the water. Early in the play Broadbent tries to explain about Letchworth to his bibulous Irish friend Tim Haffigan:

Broadbent: Have you ever heard of Garden City?
Tim (doubtfully): D'ye mane Heavn?
Broadbent: Heaven! No: it's near Hitchin.

Shaw had been sent Ebenezer Howard's book when it came out, and said to himself, 'The same old vision.' He conceded in 1899 that 'an artificial city, so to speak, is no more impossible than a canal is: in fact Eastbourne & many other places are such cities; but the thing should be kept clear of philanthropy & utopian socialism because people (the tenants) will not stand being kept in a nursery'. A couple of months later he did speak in public in support of the Garden City project after a lecture given by Ebenezer Howard, but noted in his speech that a scheme of some kind similar to Howard's was brought to his notice at least once every seven years.[3]

Long before Shaw came on the scene, there was an odd social experiment in Hertfordshire of the kind to which he was referring. An

Irishman, Feargus O'Connor (1794–1855), the MP for Cork and a noted Chartist leader and radical until he lost his seat due to his belief in direct action, bought, in 1846, 103 acres of land at Heronsgate near Chorleywood. He had a utopian plan for resettling in the countryside, as smallholders, artisans from manufacturing towns in the north of England. Seventy thousand people subscribed to his Chartist Land Co., and the plots at Heronsgate – between two and four acres, each with a substantial cottage and outhouses – were allocated by lottery.[4]

The lucky winners had to pay rent, but since they were tailors, cobblers and so on by training, all strangers to one another, and knew nothing about farming, they did not make enough money to cover their rent, let alone make a proper livelihood. Even if they had been more experienced, the Heronsgate experiment couldn't have worked. The holdings were too small to make it worthwhile keeping a horse and plough.

The project had to be subsidized from O'Connor's own pocket, accounts were badly kept, and after only five years the company was declared bankrupt and the plots were sold off. The disillusioned artisans returned to the industrial north and the hope of regular wages.

O'Connor himself, who was back in Parliament as the Member for Nottingham, 'began to conduct himself in a disorderly manner in the House of Commons', and in 1852 was found to be of unsound mind by a commission of lunacy.[5] The houses he built at Heronsgate have survived as desirable residences in commuterland. The names of the roads – off Long Lane, squashed between modern Chorleywood and the M25 – bear witness to the home towns of the unsuccessful pioneers: Bradford Road, Halifax Road, Stockport Road, Nottingham Road.

It's important to get nostalgia under control before it runs away with us. Hertfordshire's stubborn residual loveliness – its curving fields, its wedges of woodland, its villages and market towns – is man-made. That is why it is lovable. We are so used to learning that human beings ruin everything natural they meddle with that it is reassuring to see evidence of our long participation in an organic, functioning environment. You cannot stop in Braughing, or Westmill, or Benington, or Aldbury, or stand in the elegiac yew-clotted churchyard sloping down to the river at Great Amwell, without recognizing a genius for gentle domestic and sacred architecture and the proper use of land and landscape.

But everything old and mellow that now delights the eye was once offensively new. Lionel M. Munby, author of *The Hertfordshire Landscape*, is our best mentor here. There was ribbon development, he reminds me, along the Icknield Way before the Romans came: the 'intensity of settlement' along its now lonely tracts must have been 'quite remarkable'. Roman Verulamium was a planned town, and the site of St Albans 'was as much the result of a conscious human choice as is the location of Garden Cities and New Towns'. Royston too was a 'new town' – it is not mentioned in Domesday at all. The attractive main streets of Buntingford or Redbourn, built in the coaching era, were once brash and new, 'with decaying and abandoned settlements in the countryside behind them'.[6]

As new houses, shops and inns grew up on the main roads, old churches were often left high and dry. Sometimes disastrous fires, or epidemics such as plague or the Black Death, caused villages to be deserted. The Black Death killed fifty priests in Hertfordshire, plus an Abbot of St Albans and forty-seven monks. (Dead ordinary folk weren't generally worth counting. But there are fourteenth-century graffiti in Ashwell Church testifying to their terror and misery.) Hertfordshire is studded with deserted villages, some of them leaving no evidence of their existence other than lumps in the fields, and a piece of moat.

The one that touches me most is Caldecote, only half a mile off the A1(M) near the Bedfordshire border, given deceptive importance by its very own signpost from the motorway. It's more interesting to approach it from the south-east on foot up the narrow road – a former field-track – from Newnham, Reginald Hine's birthplace.

Caldecote's existence has been tenuous but stubborn. There was an early Roman settlement round here. According to Pevsner, the village was 'mostly deserted' already in the early fifteenth century. That can't be right. Some of the woodwork and plate in the church dates from after that period. In the south porch of the church is a famous canopied and crocketed stoup, but the doors were locked when we visited so we did not see it.

What we did see was the sad little grey church of St Mary Magdalene, surrounded up to its locked door by vigorous nettles and thistles. There is no path up to it, and it stands in the yard of a no-nonsense working farm; there is an ugly farmhouse of yellow brick, and a short row of unremarkable cottages in the lane beyond. The wide, high fields around thrum with the sound of tractors. Close by on the ground are the remains of another house or houses – rubble, loose masonry, foundations. There are piles of assorted scrap, and a clapped-out car atop the scrap. The most modern map available still marks the manor house. But it's not there. Caldecote has been disintegrating faster in recent years.

The last lords of the manor are the Inskips; Wickham Inskip, a gentleman farmer, was a friend of Reginald Hine. His nephew, the first Viscount Caldecote, a Bristol man and successively a Conservative MP, Attorney-General, defence minister and Lord Chief Justice, died in 1947 and is buried in the overgrown churchyard. His son the second Viscount Caldecote lives in Hampshire.

Caldecote's struggle to survive can be traced through succeeding waves of local historians. When Domesday was compiled there were nine villeins, four cottagers, and a priest. In Elizabeth I's time the place belonged to the Hale family, and there are Hales in the grave-yard. Chauncy in 1700 described Caldecote as 'situated in the Champion', i.e. in the open fields, and referred to the manor house, the rectory, and four cottages. A pilgrim in 1931 remarked on the farmer's pigs rooting around in the neglected graveyard.[7] When Arthur Mee was here in 1940 there was no motor road through at all, and there was still the sixteenth-century rectory and great thatched barns, spanning two sides of the churchyard, dwarfing the church.[8] In 1953 the population was forty-four. The church was not made redundant until 1975. The *Shell Guide to Hertfordshire*, published in 1982, describes the ancient barns at Caldecote 'collapsing into wood-pulp, their thatches like sodden shredded wheat' (Welgar, presumably). There's no sign of them at all now. I went to Caldecote too late.

Why some villages decay while comparable ones survive and thrive would be the subject of another whole book. The natural neighbour of Caldecote and Newnham is Radwell, where, in the eighteenth century, the miller's daughter was so beautiful that the infatuated curate wrote her poems and people came for miles to stare at her. The miller shut her up in the house and married her off to the local carpenter. Now the A1(M) roars between Caldecote and Newnham, separating Radwell Grange, on the Caldecote side, from Radwell village. As with Caldecote, only a short stretch of lane separates the village from the motorway. It's an unpropitious situation.

Even in the 1950s W. Branch Johnson could describe Radwell as 'sequestered', and 'absolutely feudal in feeling'. The miracle is, that is still true. The houses are pretty and cared for. Money is spent on them. The lane slopes down to a bridge over the Ivel, which swells on one side into a great lake. There are ducks and swans and, in the gardens, an extraordinary consensus that the thing to do is to grow bright red tulips.

What is now Old Stevenage, on the former Great North Road, was a development that left St Nicholas's Church stranded, but not abandoned, on higher ground half a mile away. Generally speaking, only when a new church was built on the new high street was the old one left to fall into ruins.

One example among many is at Thundridge, just north of Ware on the A10. The old church is where the original village was, half a mile east of the main road and beside the river Rib (into which St Thomas à Becket once fell, to be rescued by the local miller). A traveller investigating in 1931 called Thundridge old church 'a most depressing sight, a ghastly derelict'; he stumbled over 'heaps of debris and the hoofmarks of the vandal'.[9]

We walked up the footpath through the fields that leads from modern Thundridge towards the hamlet of Cold Christmas past the old church on a sunny Easter Sunday. Lots of other people had the same idea, it was like a pilgrimage. Only the roofless tower of the old church remains, and tombstones at all angles like bad teeth. But there was no debris, no hoofmarks of the vandal, and it was pleasant to see so many local people walking to the ruin, as if they were visiting an elderly relative in hospital.

What happens now, it seems to me, is that we care for most of our antiquities; and 'settlements', whether old or not so old, will never again be abandoned, until our civilization falls (as all do in the end), or unless there should be some nuclear or chemical disaster that makes not only Hertfordshire but the rest of England uninhabitable. There will just be more and more building. In any case, an 'abandoned' New Town would be a sort of nightmare. Modern materials do not decay gracefully.

But disasters apart, it is unlikely to happen. Living space is too precious to be let go. New and old fight for the same air. Developers fly in helicopters over Hertford, Barbara Cartland, who lives near Essendon, told me, and when they see any kind of a space between the houses they swoop down and offer tens of thousands for the site.

The novelist E. M. Forster (1879–1970), like John Betjeman, hated what was happening to Hertfordshire in his lifetime. Forster's father died before he was two, and he lived with his mother until he was fourteen just outside Stevenage in a rented house called Rook's Nest, up the winding lane above St Nicholas's Church. In later life he looked back with sentimental affection on his Hertfordshire years. Rook's Nest itself was the model for the house Howards End, in the great novel of that name published in 1910, in which Stevenage itself is called Hilton, and Hertfordshire is described as 'England meditative'.

I used to read and re-read *Howards End* for its own sake before ever I saw or knew about Rook's Nest. Mrs Wilcox in the book, who lives at Howards End, was modelled on Mrs Poston, a friend of Forster's mother who took the house after the Forsters left; her daughter Elizabeth Poston, one of the few women whom Forster really liked, became a distinguished composer and lived on at Rook's Nest/Howards End, with her dog and her donkeys, until her death in 1986.

Old Miss Poston, whom we used to see quite often, was fiercely protective of her family's Forster connection: she declined to give any help to Forster's biographer P. N. Furbank. There used to be a splendid junk-cum-antique shop in Baldock run by an Irishman called Mr Geary, where half the neighbourhood would be met rummaging around for bargains on Saturday mornings, and where we bought a good many cheap and interesting things for the cottage. Among them were three old bentwood chairs of bizarre country design, with oddly arched backs and rectangular caned seats. They came from Rook's Nest, sold to Mr Geary by Miss Poston. We were very pleased with the chairs, and liked to think they might have been a familiar sight to

Forster. (They now belong to Hugo, my son and the photographer.) We told Miss Poston that we had bought them, thinking she would be pleased to know they were appreciated. But it was an insensitive thing to do. She was embarrassed.

In 1946, when Stevenage New Town was beginning to be built, E. M. Forster broadcast a talk called 'A Challenge for Our Time'.[10] He said:

> I was brought up as a boy in one of the home counties, in a district which I still think the loveliest in England. There is nothing special about it – it is agricultural land, and could not be described in terms of beauty spots. It must always have looked much the same. I have kept in touch with it, going back to it as to an abiding city and still visiting the house which was once my home, for it is occupied by friends. A farm is through the hedge, and when the farmer there was eight years old and I was nine we used to jump up and down on his grandfather's straw ricks and spoil them . . . Life went on there as usual until this spring.

Now, he told his listeners, 'a satellite town for sixty thousand people is to be built. The people now living and working there are doomed; it is death in life for them and they move in a nightmare.' The best agricultural land was being taken, and compensation was inadequate. 'Anyhow, the satellite town has finished them off as completely as it will obliterate the ancient and delicate scenery. Meteorite town would be a better name. It has fallen out of the sky.'

But Forster knew that 'people must have houses'. He himself had working-class friends in London who badly needed to be rehoused. There was in 1946, as there still is, a genuine dilemma. Forster blamed the 'scientists' – he meant social scientists and planners – and, even more, the short-term vision of central government. The scientist, he said in this broadcast, 'is subsidized by the terrified governments who need his aid, pampered and sheltered so long as he is obedient, and prosecuted under Official Secrets Acts when he is naughty'. For 'scientist' read 'civil servant', and those words apply to the late 1980s as neatly as they did to the late 1940s.

Forster did not think that Rook's Nest would survive. Nearly forty years on, it is still there behind its wall and blue-painted gate, and so is the farm next door, even though an arm of New Stevenage almost touches it. I walked up to Rook's Nest with the dog in the week I heard that Miss Poston had died. She had put a plaque on the front of the house, giving her mother's dates, and E. M. Forster's, and her own – with a space left for the date of her death. It all looked very quiet and sad, from the neglected garden to the aged curtains in the windows, lined with dark-blue material worn to shreds.

We have been up there again more recently. Her donkeys still stand patiently in the paddock, and though the vine and the wych-elm that Forster loved have gone and the lichen-covered dovecote is empty, the house is alive again, inherited by Elizabeth Poston's nephew and his family. The fields beyond are now officially known as 'Forster Country', and may escape development.

If they do, they may be the only fields round here that will. The Green Belt, everywhere, is being what they call 'adjusted' or 'redefined'. As I write, it has been announced that a new 'mini-town' of 1,600 houses, plus associated services, is going to be built on 273 acres of agricultural land between the present New Stevenage boundary and the village of Weston. This will encircle 'Forster Country' and come very close to Graveley. From our upstairs windows we look across the saucer in which the pond lies to the high field on the other side of the road where, on summer evenings, the village cricket team plays. Instead of the tiny silhouettes of cricketers, we could soon be seeing the red roofs of new houses.

As Forster said, people must have houses. The *average* waiting time for families on New Stevenage's council housing list is six years, and the number of council houses diminishes as tenants become owner-occupiers. In the county as a whole there are around 350 homeless people in bed-and-breakfasts, and over a thousand in overcrowded conditions.[11] The 'mini-town' of private housing will not help them at all. So who wants it? Landowners who will be handsomely compensated, and the developers: Countryside Properties, Croudace Homes and Wates.

The Stevenage story is just one of many in Hertfordshire. Stephen Pile, the humorous journalist, made the recent row over another proposed development, at Bricket Wood, the subject of a funny column:

It will amaze those of you who live in proper rural places (I mean the Isle of Mull, not Hampshire, which is basically a stage-set) that here in the south-east we have convinced ourselves that we are surrounded by glorious countryside – Surrey and Hertfordshire. This is a reference to the green belt, a stretch of dusty old grass bordered by motorways and subject to constant encroachment.

It is the general, if simplified, view of the government that the green belt would be infinitely more attractive if it were turned into one huge drive-in supermarket. But we country folk are putting our foot down here.

Last week Bricket Wood, an old-world haven of rustic charm that nestles peacefully between the M1, the M10 and the M25, was causing much publicized ructions at a Hertfordshire planning inquiry to preserve its 'rural way of life'.[12]

He could have been even funnier about poor Bricket Wood, a village of about five thousand inhabitants, had he known that it used to be a mecca for naturists, or nudists. In the 1920s and 1930s there were eight flourishing nudist colonies here, sustaining themselves on fruit and nuts from the woods and holding health classes.

It was not local farmers but the Department of Transport, incidentally, that stood to make a profit – about £50 million – from the Bricket Wood development. They bought up the Green Belt land in question in 1982 in connection with the construction of the M25, before anyone imagined that planning permission would ever be given.[13] In the event, it was not; the scheme was turned down in February 1989.

The only bit of Hertfordshire that can't easily be worked into a concrete and red-brick knitting pattern is East Anglian Hertfordshire – my favourite part, the north-eastern bulge, where the county boundaries are with Cambridgeshire and north Essex. This area, only about fifteen miles across in any direction, is bounded by Royston and Ware to the north and south, and by Stevenage and Bishop's Stortford to the west and east, with that spider's web of lanes and villages between. The A10 – based on Roman Ermine Street – bisects it, and Buntingford is the largest town, if indeed it is a town.

Look at the map, and imagine what will happen to the rest of Hertfordshire if restrictions continue to be relaxed and the developers have their way. We have no airport of our own, but expanding businesses are well served by Luton on one side and Stanstead on the other. Stevenage, whose expanding shopping corridor to the south is already creeping close to Knebworth, could soon grow out northwards to join Letchworth, which is already separated from Hitchin by little more than Harkness the rose-growers, and from Baldock just by the motorway. This would be the 'urban area' of North Herts.

Knebworth, about to be engulfed from the north by this putative urban area, is also being fingered by Welwyn Garden City from the south; and Welwyn–Hatfield is very nearly a unit already. Hatfield and St Albans are kept apart only by an airfield and some sand and gravel pits; nothing that couldn't be 'adjusted'. That takes care of the middle of the county as well as the north. Five miles south of Hatfield you are approaching Potters Bar, and London. Nothing very substantial keeps St Albans and Hemel Hempstead from one another or from the tangle of Watford, and London.

In the south-east, Hertford-and-Ware – as they are often designated, administratively – are getting closer to Hoddesdon and the unbroken string of Lea Valley towns, and London. In the south-west, the A41 is already built up for virtually all its length; ribbon development only has to become Green Belt development for Rickmansworth, Chorleywood and their satellite villages to join the Hemel Hempstead–Watford sprawl, and London.

That takes care of more or less the whole county.

4

ROMANS

To make a long story short ... Around the time of the birth of Christ, the area later called Hertfordshire was thickly wooded, especially in the south-east. You can visit something very like that ancient woodland carefully preserved at Hoddesdon Park Wood, just west of the A10; Red Hills track, following the course of the Roman Ermine Street, runs through it.

In the woods lived Belgic tribes who had come from Gaul about 350 years earlier, pushing some of the Celts out. The chief tribe around here, at least south of the river Lea, was the Catuvellauni.

Archaeologists have remarked on the very rough workmanship of the prehistoric tools found in these parts. I regret to report that 'the earliest evidence of the presence of man in the district which is now known as Hertfordshire seems to point to the fact that the dweller in this region was somewhat inferior in intelligence to the inhabitants of other districts, as for example Sussex'.[1] Hertfordshire people, in modern times, have been called – and have called themselves – 'Hertfordshire Hedgehogs'. It suggests a population slow, amiable, well defended and apt to be overrun, or to be run over.

When Caesar made his second and successful attempt at invasion, in 54 BC, the powerful king of the Catuvellauni tribe, Cassivellaunus, was in charge of defence. He could not prevent the Romans crossing the Thames; they had found collaborators among the treacherous

Trinovantes from Essex. He temporarily checked their advance, but could not stop them penetrating further, towards what is now St Albans. Cassivellaunus and his men were chased into the woods, and sued for peace.

It's said that Cassivellaunus's fateful defeat took place in the modern outskirts of Wheathampstead at the Devil's Dyke, an ancient British entrenchment which was part of the fortifications of a settlement; presumably the Slad, another piece of entrenchment half a mile away on the other side of Beech Hyde Lane, was part of the same fortification system. The Devil's Dyke is deep, shaded with trees, and pleasant to walk in. It used to be private property. A notice at the entrance informs the visitor that Lord Brocket presented the dyke to the public to commemorate the coronation of King George VI and Queen Elizabeth – now the queen mother, and a Hertfordshire girl in spite of her Scottishness: she was born and partly brought up at St Paul's Walden Bury.

Cassivellaunus's son, Tasciovanus, got the better of the men of Essex, if not of the Romans. He was the first prince to put inscriptions on local coins, which were struck at Verulamium. His son, Cunobelinus (Shakespeare's Cymbeline), ruled over south-east Britain from his seat at Colchester. But the tribal kings were always quarrelling among themselves instead of fighting the Romans. Caractacus, another troublesome son of the Catuvellauni, was defeated by the Roman emperor Claudius, and south-east Britain was subjugated until the rising of the Iceni under Queen Boadicea, whom it is more scholarly to call Queen Boudicca, in AD 62.

I think that's more or less how it was. Verulamium (Roman St Albans) was the chief Roman town in Hertfordshire, but there were other important stations, such as the one near Braughing, where Ermine Street and Stane Street intersect. There was a Roman town at Hitchin. Roman remains have been found all over the county, notably at Ashwell and Welwyn; in the excavations for the building of Welwyn Garden City huge quantities of Roman artefacts were uncovered. In the tumulus on Limlow Hill, just over the border in Cambridgeshire, skeletons with coins struck in the time of Claudius and Vespasian have been found. Roman pottery – urns, jars, dishes – was found neat the Norman motte and bailey at Great Wymondley in the 1880s, and the remains of a farmstead or villa, with a magnificent mosaic floor, less than a mile away near the river Purwell on the outskirts of modern Hitchin. There was also evidence of a Roman cemetery.

But Verulamium was the flagship city, and in Verulamium every citizen, including the natives, was automatically given the status of a citizen of Rome. *Civis romanus sum*. Boudicca was every bit as tough with these Romanized Britons as she was with the Romans.

Queen Boudicca was not a Hertfordshire girl. She came from Essex, and she and her men overwhelmed both Roman Colchester and Verulamium in a revolt against the occupying power – incited, as the greatest early historian of the county, Sir Henry Chauncy, writes, 'by the deep Love she bore to her Country, and exasperated by the bitter Hatred she had to the Romans'. A Roman historian, Dion Cassius, left a terrifying account of her, exaggerated perhaps in order to explain how she had managed to pull it off. He described her as being 'of the largest size, most terrible of aspect, most savage of countenance, most harsh of voice; having a profusion of yellow hair, which hung down to her hips; and wearing a large golden collar, a parti-coloured floating vest drawn close about her bosom, over this a thick mantle connected by a clasp, and in her hand a spear'.

She massacred, tortured and crucified her prisoners. The women were stripped, and their breasts cut off and stuffed in their mouths, after which their mouths were sewn up. Or so Dion Cassius says. Then the Roman governor, Suetonius, who had been away in Anglesea while this was going on, returned and beat her off.

The last Roman legions left in the early fifth century. Hertfordshire and the surrounding counties were under threat from the Saxons, and the Romans told the Britons to see to their own defence – thus pulling out at a time when violence and disunity were inevitable, as is the way of decaying empires. They seem to have ignored parts of the county all along – there is no record of Roman occupation in the enclave now marked by the villages of Kimpton, Whitwell, Preston, Offley and Lilley. Very few of the Romans in Britain by the fourth century were Roman at all, anyway – the occupying forces and the administrators came from all parts of the far-flung and by now decadent empire.

Christianity had already come to England a hundred years before that, and St Alban was martyred in AD 303. Alban was the first English martyr, in so far as he was English at all. He was a soldier in Diocletian's army, and Diocletian was having a blitz against Christianity in Britain. Alban illegally sheltered a Christian and was converted by him. He was arrested wearing his new friend's clothes, in an attempt to save him. When Alban refused to worship the Roman gods, he was beheaded. The legend is that his executioner was converted on the spot, and met the same fate.

But in general Hertfordshire was Romanized rather than oppressed; and danger came from the brigands, immigrants and pirates from Denmark, Gaul and Germany, who were always as much a threat to the 'Roman' authorities as to the native population. What we call 'Roman villas' were often the property of prosperous, landowning Romanized Britons. The Roman settlements in this county were generally on the sites of ancient British settlements; and after the legions left, some were taken over by succeeding waves of invaders who either were assimilated or moved on.

A continuity of settlement, from the earliest times to today, seems more basic to our history than the political and dynastic upheavals of the textbooks. Many 'Roman' soldiers and officials had married over here, and their descendants went native. Romanized Britons, if they had land, carried on much as before, in so far as they could, after the legions left; and I like to think of poor people climbing over the neglected walls of the deserted homes of former imperial administrators, and running back to their wooden houses in the forest clearings with loot. A chunk of mosaic, a broken tablet with an inscription, a scrap of papyrus, a glazed bowl, a ragged wall-hanging, a basket of mulberries, cuttings or roots of apricots and vines.

The continuity is obvious from our older buildings. Nowadays, we have a nostalgic respect for the past. We preserve, conserve, catalogue and label the handiwork of our ancestors. Anything else is seen as vandalism. But our forebears appropriated the past, and assimilated it into their present.

Verulamium fell into ruins. But early medieval down-and-outs squatted in the rubble, and when the first Norman abbot of St Albans was rebuilding the eighth-century abbey built by Offa, King of Mercia, to glorify St Alban, he used the old Roman city as a quarry –

and not only for the abbey. Churches and great houses around incorporate lumps of Roman stone and flat Roman bricks into their fabric. (Tiles and bricks were much the same thing until the fifteenth century). As late as the eighteenth century cartloads of Roman bricks from Verulamium were being used for mending the highways.

This mentality prevailed until pious antiquarianism took its place. In Harpenden in the 1820s a stone Roman coffin was being used as a farmyard water-trough until it was spotted and whipped off to the British Museum. In Aldenham, before the church was restored in 1840, villagers were casually removing parts of it for their cottages; they used tombstones for doorsteps and hearthstones, and an Aldenham baker used them, inscription side up, as the floor of his bread oven, so that your loaf came out with 'Sacred to the Memory' embossed on the bottom. In another Hertfordshire parish, the vicar paved his pigsty with tombstones taken from the churchyard. One parishioner complained that his own father's headstone had been 'borrowed' for this purpose. 'I am told, on good authority, that the tombstones are still in the same indecent place', wrote John Edwin Cussans in 1881.[2]

It's still hard to date Hertfordshire houses, since the very oldest are often encrusted with later plasterwork, or have wings and additions which conceal the lines of the primitive structure. Cottered Lordship, for example, has been claimed as the oldest dwelling house in the county, but you would not guess it to look at it. Conversely, the newest portions of older village houses are often built in traditional styles, with traditional exterior finishes such as decorative plasterwork – pargeting or 'combed work' – and roofed with thin, flat Hertfordshire tiles salvaged from some irretrievably broken-down cottage. Tiles, bricks and pottery were made locally from the Roman occupation onwards, as village names attest: Potters Bar, Potters Crouch, Potters Green, Potters Heath, Potten End.

Today's building work still brings the distant past to light. In the newest area of New Stevenage, the Chells Manor estate, the developers have recently unearthed a grey pottery jar containing 2,500 silver Roman coins covering a seventy-year period from AD 193 to 263 – probably the life–savings of the owner of the timber-built farmstead which, from the evidence, then stood on the site. He would have hidden the money in order to avoid the punitive imperial taxes, raised to defend the area against marauders. When the A1(M) was being built, a Roman bathhouse of about AD 250 was discovered close to Old Welwyn. It has been preserved in a steel vault under the motorway, with access from the A1000 roundabout – the only one of its kind preserved in such a manner in Britain.

The Roman theatre at Verulamium was for a long time the only one known about in England, and thus is very famous. It was first uncovered in 1847, but was not excavated until the 1930s. It is on the Gorhambury estate, on the western fringe of St Albans, separated from the modern city by the A414 ring road. Gorhambury belongs to the Earl of Verulam, whose Gorhambury Estates Company financed the excavations and administer the remains.

The theatre was first built in the middle of the second century, probably in association with the religious rites of a temple that stood nearby. It had a circular central area with banked seats all round except where the circle was interrupted by a small stage with a changing-room behind it. Improvements and alterations were made during the decades of the Roman occupation; there is evidence that by the fourth century the theatre was abandoned, and used as the town tip.

Roman Watling Street ran through Verulamium under a great gateway, following the course of what is now Lord Verulam's drive, parallel to the former Great North Road (which rejoins the route of Watling Street as it runs in a straight line north-west to Redbourn). Where the street ran past the theatre there were rows of shops for jewellers and metalworkers. A second-century town house has also been excavated; it had central heating in three of its rooms, and a fine mosaic floor with a dolphin design, and painted walls.

The most pleasant way to approach the remains of Verulamium is down St Albans's Fishpool Street; a long, tight, narrow Jane-Austenish street of small houses dating from the sixteenth to the early nineteenth centuries, many of them timbered, with overhanging upper storeys and high doorsteps. Towards the bottom on the left is St Michael's Manor, which belonged to the same family for five hundred years before becoming an agreeable and comfortable hotel, with the river Ver flowing through its garden. Fishpool Street bends left into St Michael's Street and bridges the Ver at Kingsbury Mill, which is now a museum; then you cross the ring road and gain access to the Roman theatre from the entrance to the Gorhambury estate.

The Roman city, in its various phases of development, covered an area of nearly two hundred acres – to the left and right of Fishpool Street, as well as on the Gorhambury site, where it adjoined a former stronghold of the Catuvellauni in Prae Wood. Some of Verulamium is buried under the ring road. Half a mile to the left, in the direction of Hemel Hempstead, the ring road crosses the course of the Roman city wall: you can see long humps in the green fields on either side.

There were suburban Roman homesteads too, well outside the city walls. Some are known about, some doubtless lie undiscovered, some are lost. At Park Street (which is not a city street but a village on Watling Street, between St Albans and Radlett), a German refugee schoolboy during the Second World War noticed bits of a building in a gravel pit; they were a Roman villa. Because the gravel was urgently needed, and there were no available archaeologists, the villa was examined, photographed – and destroyed.[3] (Where a Hertfordshire village name has the suffix 'Street', it means the road through or beside it was paved at a time when most roads were not; which frequently suggests an originally Roman highway.)

I have to say that the Roman theatre, as it is now presented, is a frightful disappointment to me, though a local historian has praised it as 'one of the best and most pleasing acts of restitution that exist'.[4] There is very little to see. Low flint walls mark the outlines. A single column (reconstructed) is the only object that breaks the horizontals. The sites of the metalworkers' shops are bare earth rectangles demarcated by low cement boundaries. They could be seed-beds, or graves, or nothing at all. The visitors plod round, a little bewildered, their imaginations strained but not satisfied, and wonder whether it was worth the 8op entrance ticket.

Most of what was uncovered has been taken into the Verulamium Museum opposite St Michael's Church on the St Albans side of the ring road. The dolphin mosaic is here, and chunks of painted wall, scale models, and quantities of coins, tools, pottery, glass, jewellery and other artefacts mainly from the excavations of Verulamium but also from other sites in the vicinity. It is here that one gets an idea of the richness and complexity of the civilization the Romans brought to Britain.

Perhaps because their remote ancestors were once citizens of Rome, the people of St Albans have always stood up for their rights. In the medieval period the town prospered. There has been a famous school in the abbey precincts since the eleventh century, and the third printing press in all England was established at this school, which is one of the three oldest grammar schools in England. There are about eight books in existence which claim to have been printed in St Albans between 1479 and 1486. The Benedictine abbey with its monks also maintained two leper hospitals, owned or leased from the Crown many manors, and was the town's richest and most powerful employer.

It was not the only religious institution in the town. Down Cottonmill Lane, close to the river Ver downstream from Verulamium, stood Sopwell Nunnery, founded in 1140 for a small number of women under Benedictine rule, apparently on the site of an even earlier hermitage for pre-Christian holy women. Chauncy writes that this twelfth-century foundation came about when 'two religious Women made a poor House by wradling of the Boughs of Trees with Rods, and covering it with Bark'. When their chastity, piety and 'laudable and unchangeable Behaviour for many Years' was made known to the then abbot, he 'commanded that convenient Houses should be erected for the Women, and appointed that they should be clothed with Vests after the Manner of Nuns ... and that none should be taken into their Colledge, but a select and limited Number of Virgins'. The surviving ruin is not the nunnery, but the remains of a sixteenth-century house. (And further down Cottonmill Lane, over the river, is yet another manor house converted into a hotel, the Sopwell House Hotel.) Dame Juliana Berners, the alleged and un-nunlike author of the fifteenth-century *Book of St Albans* (all about heraldry, hawking and hunting, with a treatise on 'Fishing with an Angle' in a later edition), is said to have been a nun at Sopwell. Serious scholars do not credit this; but the book was certainly printed on the St Alban press.

Students of trade union history should study the history of St Albans, where some of the earliest known industrial action took place. In the thirteenth and fourteenth centuries the citizens insisted on their rights as freemen and on their 'common rights', which is to say that they would not accept that all the land and woods around belonged to the abbot. But successive abbots treated them as villeins, taking tolls and enforcing labour in the abbey mills and fields. The men of St Albans held protest meetings, marched on the abbey, went to London to gain support, and formed themselves into an early Friendly Society. They had paid leaders, a common fund, and were well organized. The rows went on for generations.

The fortieth abbot's religious and secular power was broken, after a struggle, by Henry VIII in 1539. According to Chauncy, 'the Abbot and Convent of this Monastery, through Fear, surrender'd to the King all their rich Monastery, with all Revenues belonging to it', handing over their great seal – and, presumably, their jewels and rich stuffs and precious plate – to the sinister gentlemen called 'the King's Visitors'. The abbot was given a pension of £266 13s 4d for life, which was not ungenerous. The ordinary monks got pensions of between £33 and £6 a year.

The fabric of the abbey was spared; the townspeople bought the shell for £400. They then used the precincts as a short cut, treading paths through the abbey itself. In the seventeenth century it was used as a military prison for defeated royalists; their names are among those scratched on the pillars and walls. In the eighteenth century it continued to be neglected, though services were still held in it. The fourteenth-century gatehouse, with its dungeons, was a prison for French soldiers during the Napoleonic Wars.

From Roman Verulamium, you can see the Norman towers of the great church which was built over Offa's eighth-century abbey, rising on its hill above sprawling modern St Albans. What you cannot tell is how much that view owes to the restoration of the 1870s. This enormous undertaking was financed by the first Lord Grimthorpe, who lived just on the other side of Watling Street from Gorhambury at Batchwood Hall (now the golf club), a house he designed himself.

Grimthorpe was a most eccentric man, a lawyer, a mathematician, and a professional controversialist. His passions were clocks and bells – he wrote a book on clocks, watches and bells, with an appendix on weathercocks; he designed the clock for the Great Exhibition of 1851, which was later installed in King's Cross Station, and he prepared the specifications for Big Ben at Westminster.

For the restoration of St Alban's, he hired the architect Sir George Gilbert Scott, but interfered with the plans all the way down the line. Scott said that his patron, who was tall and 'stern of aspect', had 'such an unpleasant way of doing things that he makes one hate one's best work'.[5] But the fact remains that Grimthorpe put more than £130,000 of his own money (he made a fortune as a barrister) into St Alban's Abbey, which was granted cathedral status soon after completion of the restoration.

When you stand in the sloping place called Romeland, with its trees and graveyard – where George Tankerfield, in the reign of Bloody Mary, was burnt alive in 1555 – in the lee of the massive building (second only to Winchester in length among the English cathedrals), it is easy to forget Lord Grimthorpe. But the west front is almost entirely the work of his restoration, as is the great round window in the wall of the north transept, and the five lancet windows in the south transept. Another local peer, Lord Aldenham, also contributed to the late-nineteenth-century restoration; the fifteenth-century stone screen behind the altar, with its intricate canopies and rows of little figures in tiered niches, had been battered and broken ever since Henry VIII's 'visitors' got rid of the fortieth abbot. With Aldenham money, the screen was renewed.

It has been fashionable to sneer at St Alban's Cathedral. Pevsner (or his assistants, on whom he leaned heavily for his volume on Hertfordshire) calls it 'joyless', on account of its dark Roman bricks, the heaviness of its proportions, and its architectural bastardy. Its 'peculiar architectural history', he writes, has deprived it of visual attractiveness. I do not think this is fair. Its weight and height give the county as a whole its central focal point. This cathedral wears its dramatic history and the vicissitudes through which it has passed openly, like an overweight prizefighter. The solid efficiency of the Norman conquerors, caught in time between the grandiose aspirations of two great empires – that of Rome and that of Victorian Britain, coexist in its fabric and its forms.

* * *

Nevertheless there is a place here that I like better than the cathedral. It is Gorhambury, in the grounds of which the disappointing Roman theatre lies. This manor had originally, like everything else for miles around, belonged to the Abbot of St Alban's. But in the reign of Elizabeth I it was acquired by Sir Nicholas Bacon, a man, according to Chauncy, 'of great Learning, rare Wit, and deep Experience', married to 'a choice Lady, exquisitely skilled for a Woman, in the Greek and Latin Tongues', who was sister-in-law to the great Cecil, Lord Burghley.

Sir Nicholas was Lord Keeper to Queen Elizabeth, who came to stay with him at Gorhambury. When she told him that his house was too small for him, he replied: 'No, Madam, but 'tis your Highness has made me too great for my House.' This was not just graceful badinage; Sir Nicholas, it is said, was so fat that he could hardly walk from Westminster Hall to the Star Chamber.

Sir Nicholas and his choice Lady were the parents of Sir Francis Bacon, 'the Glory of his Age and Nation' as Chauncy says, and one of Hertfordshire's most glitteringly ambitious sons. He went to St Alban's School, and was a great favourite with Queen Elizabeth as a boy; but when he grew up she was tough with him. She probably assessed him rightly. He betrayed the Earl of Essex, who was his friend, and sent Raleigh to his death. He was adept at the art of flattery, and unscrupulous in seeking his own advancement. After the queen's death, in his middle age, he was Attorney-General and Lord Keeper of the Great Seal under James I, and then Lord Chancellor. He was the first Lord Verulam, and Viscount St Albans.

Then he fell – he was accused of taking bribes, though it is possible it was not a matter of his own corruption so much as that of his insufficiently supervised aides. Another theory is that he accepted the bribes, and then, cynically, failed to help those who bribed him. In any case he was stripped of office, fined £40,000, imprisoned, pardoned, and devoted his remaining years to writing and to beautifying his house and garden at Gorhambury.

He had always been a writer (some people think he wrote Shakespeare's plays, which is nonsense). He was a philosopher, and in a series of works tried to formulate – in Latin – a systematic classification of all branches of knowledge. His *Essays*, written in rich, fluent, aphoristic English prose, are more fun for us. Many of his epigrams have become common quotations: 'What is truth? said jesting Pilate'; 'Men fear death, as children fear to go in the dark'; 'Revenge is a kind of wild justice'.

Fragments of his father's too-small house still stand; you reach it by continuing up the drive (which is an ordinary Hertfordshire lane). If it is not one of the days when Gorhambury is open to the public under the National Gardens Scheme, you are probably trespassing.

Past the present Gorhambury, a very substantial stone-faced eighteenth-century Palladian mansion, the lane bears left. There are meadows with sheep and a deep wooded vista ahead; and on the right, a magical ruin. It is Gorhambury Old House. Sir Nicholas built it in the 1560s; in 1787, after the new house was built, everything was demolished except the porch and part of the brick masonry of the hall and its great fireplace. But the rickety delicacy of that Renaissance porch with its columns, an inscription, and a piece of ancient jagged roof-timber sticking up into the sky like a mad finger, has a heart-breaking charm.

'Houses are built to live in, and not to look on,' wrote Francis Bacon in an essay 'Of Building', which instructs princes how to plan their palaces. But from Sir Nicholas's porch, one looks across the meadow to the white Palladian house. From the Palladian house, one looks back across the meadow at Sir Nicholas's ruin. For four hundred years these grounds have been planned to please the eye; the front of a very ordinary estate cottage further along the lane, visible from Sir Nicholas's house, has been embellished with columns and a pediment to give grace to the view.

There was once yet another great house here, for when Sir Francis Bacon came home to Gorhambury he did not live in his father's mansion but built himself a new one, and called it Verulam House; here he made his garden. He had married into money, but I do not think he loved his wife and they had no children. 'He that hath wife and children', wrote Sir Francis, 'hath given hostages to fortune; for they are impediments to great enterprises, either of virtue or mischief. Certainly the best works ... have proceeded from the unmarried or childless men.' He had a low opinion of love, asserting that 'great spirits and great business do keep out of this weak passion'.

The Icknield Way near the Bedfordshire border

Pondside Cottages, Graveley

Ruins of St Etheldreda's, Chesfield

Church Lane, between Graveley and Chesfield

The Biggin, Hitchin

Shenley Cage: 'Be Sober, Be Vigilant'

Ware: Georgian town hall, now an estate agent's

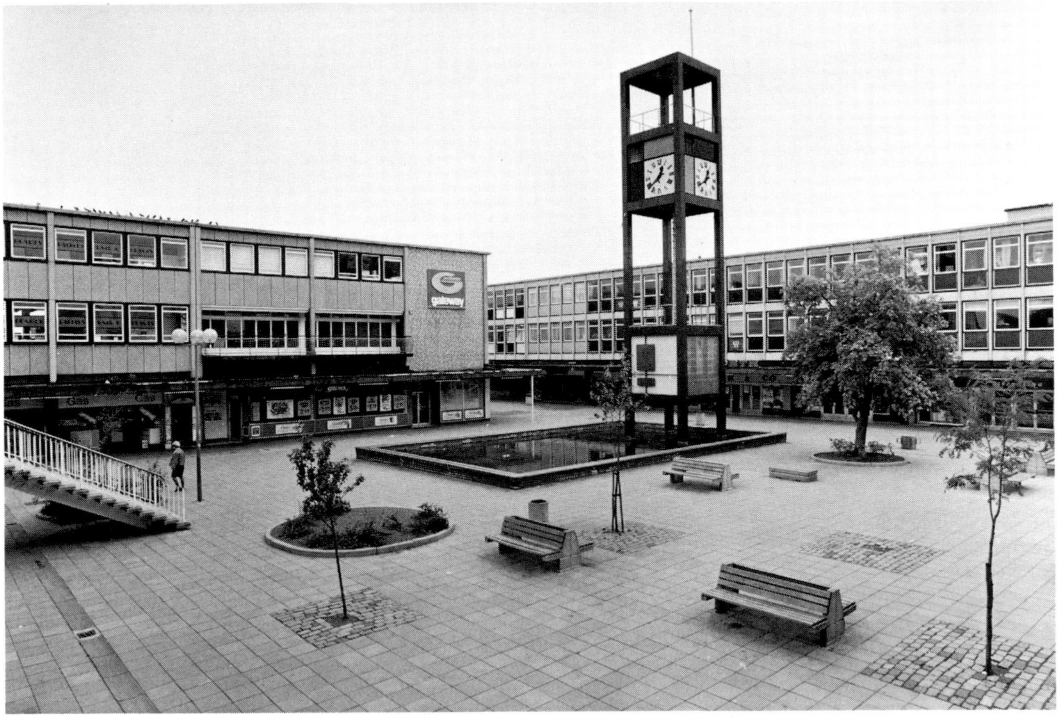
gateway

Stevenage New Town on a Sunday morning

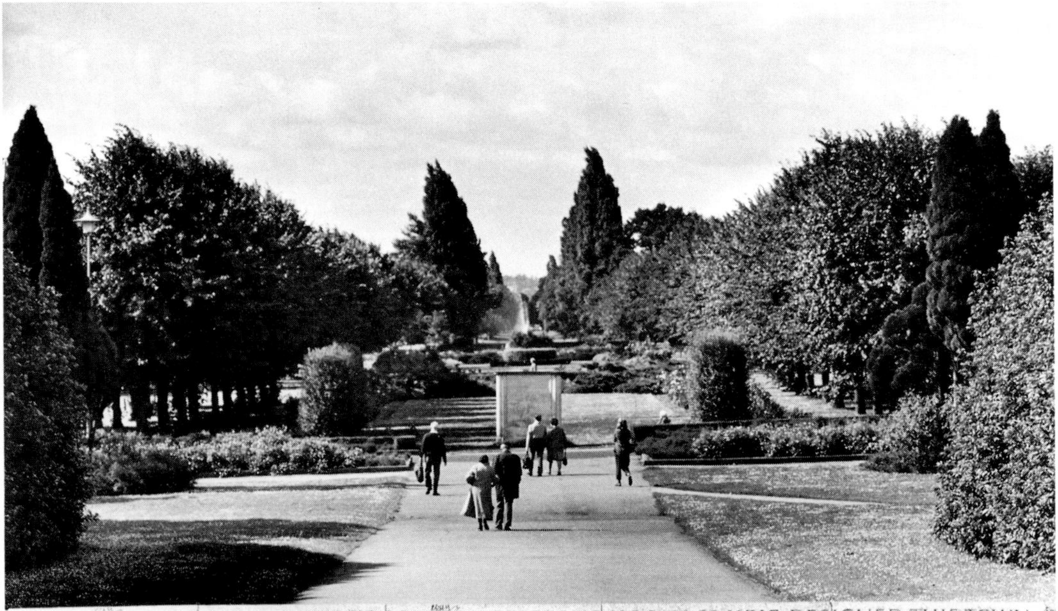
THIS GARDEN IS A MEMORIAL TO LOUIS DE SOISSONS 1890-1962 WHO DESIGNED THIS TOWN

Welwyn Garden City on a Sunday afternoon

'God Almighty first planted a garden; and, indeed, it is the purest of human pleasures.' Francis Bacon wrote his essay 'Of Gardens' at Gorhambury. If transposed – which God forbid – into modern English from his svelte and rhythmical Elizabethan prose, it would pass as a practical guide to making a grand garden and park (thirty acres, he says) today. He lists the plants to choose in order to have something in bloom or fruiting in every month of the year. He is against knot gardens, fashionable in his day; these consisted of geometrical patch-works, like a miniature maze, of differently coloured flowers, earth or stones, demarcated by low box hedges. They were designed to be best seen from a terrace or upstairs window. 'You may see as good sights many times in tarts.' He loved high hedges, arches, arbours with seats, shady walks, grassy *allées* and vistas; but he did not like topiary work, 'images cut in juniper or other garden stuff; they be for children'. He liked fountains and elaborate schemes with water, so long as the water was in movement; 'but pools mar all, they make the garden unwholesome, and full of flies and frogs'.

We can't walk round the garden that Francis Bacon made. His Verulam House was pulled down in 1663, and nothing of it remains. The garden of the eighteenth-century Gorhambury is small, by grand country house standards, but good – two acres of lawns and massive cedars, with shrub borders, a kitchen garden, a formal garden, and rolling open countryside, cross-hatched by woods, drawing the eye outwards.

Back down the drive and over the ring road, in St Michael's Church, is a monument to Francis Bacon. It is a very strange monument. He is life-size, sitting in as relaxed a way as marble allows on a chair, his head – with its wide-brimmed hat – resting on one hand; he is apparently fast asleep.

St Michael's Church has a touch of Lord Grimthorpe about the tower and the west end, but the surviving Saxon work is done with Roman bricks, and there is part of a Roman pillar under the tower. The church stands on the site of Verulamium's forum – the municipal and administrative centre of the Roman city, where the law courts were that condemned Alban to his martyrdom. In St Albans, all roads lead from Rome.

5

FOOTSTEPS

I have a special affection for the authors who have made Hert-fordshire their subject. Early local historians were gratifyingly lyrical. John Norden, in 1597, wrote that 'the aire for the most part is very salutarie, and in regard thereof many sweete and pleasant dwellings, healthfull by nature and profitable by arte and industrie, are planted there'. The 'Soyle', he said, 'is for the most part chalkie, though the upper cruste in the South and West parts be for the most part of redde earth mixed with gravell, which yet by reason of the white marle under it yeeldeth good wheat and oats'.[1]

There is also stiff London clay and gravel in the south, and pockets of plum pudding stone, or Hertfordshire Conglomerate, and 'clay-with-flints'. Fields that have been under the plough for a thousand years still throw up countless black and white flints of all shapes and sizes, which lie all over the surface of the newly turned earth. In the past, poor people were paid to collect them up. It is these flints that built Hertfordshire's churches. Sometimes the flints are large, and fantastically shaped. Some of them I carry home, for the rockery.

As for the 'chalkie' soil, it influences one's gardening. Peat-loving plants do not do well in general in Hertfordshire. This is not, for the most part, rhododendron country, though there are masses of them in the gardens of Ashridge in the north-east, and plenty in the grounds of big houses in the exceptionally prosperous pocket between Hertford and the outskirts of London. A recent phenomenon in woodlands and heaths all over the southern half of England is the 'escape' and naturalization of the common rhododendron, the mauve *Rhododendron ponticum*. This is not popular with woodland experts, since everything else dies in its immediate vicinity. It doesn't seem to mind chalkiness a bit; the exotic blooms are appearing now in our local woods.

Our immediate neighbours manage to grow heathers perfectly well too, but it doesn't seem right to me. The neighbours are from Scotland, so perhaps they need the heather to feel at home, and must be forgiven. But I agree with the gardening writer Ursula Buchan, who has written that 'Heather and conifer gardens have been spreading like a stain across our southern and midland counties, where they look as appropriate as UPVC windows in a Georgian façade.'[2]

Conifers do not look natural in this county either; when you see a fine stand of pines, you may be sure that they were planted by some wealthy landowner. The native trees are oak, beech, ash and elm – though nowadays these last are usually dead if they are standing at all, raising crazed bare limbs against the skyline. William Cobbett, on his Rural Ride through Hertfordshire in 1822, was ecstatic about the trees between Redbourn and Hemel Hempstead – 'the finest ashes I ever saw in my life. They are in great numbers and make the fields look most beautiful. No villainous things of the FIR-TRIBE offend the eye here.'

Thomas Fuller, in *The Worthies of England* (1662), wrote that 'men commonly say that such who buy a house in Hertfordshire pay two years purchase for the aire thereof'. A later historian has suggested that this is not a simple tribute to the sweet and healthy air of our county, but an ironic comment on the exorbitant prices of houses here in the seventeenth century – a complaint that can be echoed in the twentieth.

Hertfordshire's greatest early historian is Sir Henry Chauncy (1632–1719), who published his monumental *Antiquities of Hertfordshire* in 1700. He came from a family that had lived at Ardeley Bury already for several generations. His great-uncle Charles Chauncy, also of Ardeley, was the vicar of Ware when he was imprisoned in 1636 for not following Archbishop Laud's regulations about how churches should be furnished. (There were great rows at this time over things like altar rails.) Charles Chauncy, in shame, emigrated to America, where he made good and ended up as the second president of Harvard University in 1654; he had six sons who all went to Harvard. Chauncy, in America, became a revered and famous name of the highest respectability. This gives piquancy to the fact that the humble simpleton (played by Peter Sellers), whose enigmatic utterances cause him to be accepted as a wise man by the President of the United States in the film *Being There*, happened to be called Chauncy – the very name, now, being a passport to social acceptability.

Sir Henry Chauncy remained in Hertfordshire. He went to school in Bishop's Stortford, and became a lawyer, a justice of the peace, and the first recorder of the city of Hertford. His history of the county was published in an edition of 500 copies, now as 'rare as the dotteril plover' as one local historian has put it, in one vast folio volume, though later editions (very expensive) come in two volumes. It's a scholarly work, a gazetteer of every town and village. He transcribed and translated the relevant Domesday Book entries, he included family trees, personal observations, and a great deal of extraneous and often comic material. (Sometimes he made things up.) Here he is describing the flint-filled fields referred to earlier, this time in the vicinity of Flamstead, where the soil is

> exceedingly stony, insomuch that after any great Shower of Rain (by which that little Earth or Clay which is turned up by the Plow is washed below the Stones) not any thing appears, save as it were, a Heap of large rugged broken Flints, so as a Man cannot foul a Glove by rubbing on the said Soil in the dirtiest time of Winter, and yet very good Corn often grows on such Places in a dry Summer; and the Reason given for it is, because the Warmth of the Flint (having a Seed of Fire in it) preserves the Corn from the Cold in Winter ...

... and keeps it cool in summer. Meanwhile, says Chauncy, 'the stringy Fibers of the Root' pick up moisture from the soil below the stones. He also praised the dogs of Flamstead. The 'veriest curs' bred around here 'will beat the best Grey-hounds brought from elsewhere'. He was extraordinarily keen on Flamstead. It was such a healthy place, he wrote, that a woman there had lived 'to the Age of sixscore Years compleat'.

Chauncy's index is a pleasure in itself, with provocative entries such as 'Music, invention of', 'Vavasors, who?' and 'Ingfangthef, what?' The historians who followed him were not in the same class for entertainment value. The county histories of Nathaniel Salmon of Bishop's Stortford (1728), and John Edwin Cussans (1870) were useful updates and corrections of Chauncy. (Cussans was not a Hertfordshire man; but his wife came from Much Hadham.) It's not until we get to the four volumes devoted to Hertfordshire in the *Victoria History of the Counties of England*, published between 1902 and 1914, that there is anything new and important. The *Victoria Histories* are marvellous undertakings, written by a variety of hands, and covering everything from the local geology, history, industry, agriculture and economics to horse-racing and sport.

The *Victoria History* of Hertfordshire is, inevitably, a reflection of the preoccupations of its period, and this is part of the charm. There is a disproportionate amount of information about Haileybury School, Hertfordshire's major public school, including the current, i.e. 1913, cricket teams and batting averages. The various contributors disagree, giving contradictory information, scoring off one another as well as off their great predecessor Chauncy. Most of the fun to be had out of compiling these volumes was got by country gentlemen of antiquarian inclinations who had access to the great private houses; and a lot of the donkey-work of the research was done by conscientious women who had followed the Oxford Honours School of Modern History but had not taken degrees – because they were not, at that time, allowed to. Girton College, the first women's college in Cambridge, by the way, started its life in 1869 in the house next to the one my great-aunts later lived in, at Benslow on the outskirts of Hitchin.

If higher education was a man's world, so was local history. The period in which the *Victoria History* was being published was also the period of the amiable topographers such as our dear Herbert W. Tompkins, already quoted. He and his fellow writers pottered around, copying out quaint inscriptions from tombstones, dwelling lovingly on items such as stocks, whipping posts and picturesque village pumps (mostly all gone now) and indulging in exclamations such as 'What a story that round arch could tell!' (That was Mr Tompkins.)

Thank goodness they did. Any student of a region becomes aware of those who have walked that way before. They become personal acquaintances. There is no time for a thorough overview of Hertfordshire's historians, but I'd not like to pass up H. M. Alderman, author of *A Pilgrimage in Hertfordshire* (1931), whose cautious opening sentences brand him as a man who is not in danger of overstating his case: 'Is there a more historically interesting place in England than the city of St Albans? Probably not.'

Nor would I like to forget Sir William Beech Thomas, who lived at Wheathampstead. He wrote his *Hertfordshire* in 1950 and was a gentleman of the *ancien régime*. He had played cricket on the green at St Paul's Walden with Lord Strathmore, the queen mother's brother. He always seemed to have a very good time, chiefly – if I read correctly between the lines – because he had friends in the Big House of any village he visited in the course of his researches, and always got a good lunch.

One of the chief values of reading local histories spanning several centuries is in the overview afforded of the way places have changed, like time-lapse photography. The story of the Queen Eleanor Memorial at Waltham Cross is an example of what I mean. Eleanor of Castile, wife of Edward I, died in 1290 near Lincoln; the royal pair were on their way north with an army to subjugate the Scots. A portion of the queen's remains – I don't know which portion – was deposited in the Lady Chapel at Lincoln, and her heart went to the Dominican house at Blackfriars in London. What remained of her body was conveyed slowly by road to Westminster Abbey. The cortège started from Lincoln on 4 December, following an irregular route south, covering 160 miles at twelve miles per day. Afterwards, the king ordered a carved stone memorial to be built at each stopping place. In Hertfordshire, these were at St Albans and Waltham.

The one at St Albans has not survived. The nearer to London, the more elaborate the memorial; the one at Waltham Cross had its intricate decorations, and the three statues of Eleanor, carved in London and sent down to be assembled on site.

When it was first erected, this Eleanor Cross stood at the centre of a triangular green at a crossroads with no houses near it, though there was already an inn at the roadside, as there is now. By the seventeenth century the area had become built up, in a rural kind of way, and at one point a building erected right up against the memorial was ordered to be removed. Chauncy, in 1700, makes no mention of it at all. In 1795 Sir George Prescott, lord of the manor of Cheshunt (which included Waltham Cross) attempted to have the cross moved into his grounds at Theobald's Park. Luckily, this proved impossible to do.

In 1892 the cross was heavily restored, and by the time its photograph was taken for the *Victoria County History*, the grass triangle was gone and the cross was protected by new-looking railings. James Simmonds' shop stood behind it, next to the pub which still stands and retains some of its thirteenth-century timbers, and a sign spanning the street – the Four Swans, or, as it was called when Sir William Beech Thomas went there in 1950, 'Ye Olde Four Swannes Hostelrie'. 'Such gems of antiquity close to the railway, in the midst of a most modern and busy street, might supply a sentimentalist with unending subjects for his moralizings', wrote Sir William; and W. Branch Johnson, writing in 1952, felt that the cross was an introduction to Hertfordshire, coming from London. 'Not all this muddleheaded thing we call progress has succeeded in robbing Waltham Cross of its rural charm.' It has succeeded now.

The pub sign still stretches across the road, but James Simmonds' shop has gone, and the Eleanor Cross on her raised concrete triangle, behind dusty railings, is overhung by the brows of the new, bright-red brick Market Hall. The roads are narrow – too narrow for the heavy traffic they must carry. It is not a crossroads that gives much opportunity for sentimental moralizings.

A more dramatic example of the way successive accounts give a picture of the rise and fall – and sometimes the rising again – of ancient landmarks is the story of the Rye House, which is near the eastern county boundary, a couple of miles from Hoddesdon, on the edge of a maze of waterways where the Lea and the Stort meet and the New River runs alongside.

The story begins in 1683, when there was a strong moated castle, already more than a hundred years old, on this spot. There was a Protestant plot – known in the history books as the Rye House Plot – to ambush and murder Charles II and his brother James there on their way back from the races at Newmarket, in a narrow lane – which was to be blocked with an overturned cart – running past the castle outbuildings and garden wall. A maltster called Rumbold, who plied his trade in part of the Rye House, abetted the villains.

But the royal party left the races early, so the plot failed. It was leaked, and the greater men behind the would-be murderers were executed; one of them, the Earl of Essex, was arrested at Cassiobury Park, the house belonging to his family at Watford. Rumbold was hanged near the Rye House Inn opposite, and the head of one of the conspirators was stuck on the spike of the fifteenth-century gatehouse, which is the only part of the Rye House that still stands today.

Izaac Walton, pub-loving author of the *Compleat Angler*, died in the year of the Rye House Plot. There was an inn in the castle precincts even in his day; he called it 'an honest alehouse, where we shall find a cleanly room, lavender in the windows, twenty ballads stuck about the wall, and a hostess both cleanly, handsome and civil'. The Rye House seems to have alternated between grim and gay uses. Later the main building, much altered, became a workhouse.

Then in the nineteenth century the Great Bed of Ware, having been removed from the inn at Ware, was on show 'in a building in the Rye House grounds' (according to an account of 1905, when it was still there). It was either in the alehouse or in the upper room of the gatehouse itself – the former seems the more practicable – and attracted many visitors before it was taken away in 1931 to the Victoria and Albert Museum in South Kensington, where it can be seen today.

The Great Bed of Ware, nearly eleven feet square with posts eight feet high, is mentioned in Shakespeare's *Twelfth Night*, and is believed to have been made for the Fanshawe family of Ware Park. It had subsequently been in various inns at Ware, ending up at the Saracen's Head, where it was bought at a sale in 1864 by the prosperous proprietor of the Rye House.

The grounds of the Rye House had been developed as a pleasure garden, which proved so popular with the ordinary people of London that in 1848 a railway station was built specially to ferry trippers back and forth. (It is still in operation for commuters and others, the original justification long forgotten.) Cussans went there in the 1870s, and reported that 'On Easter Mondays, Whit-Monday, and Bank Holidays, the Rye House is visited by thousands of the lowest East-End roughs, with *some* respectable mechanics, but by far the largest number are decidedly objectionable.' Young people, he wrote, vied with their elders in 'intemperance and foul language. The gardens are prettily laid out and well kept. That is all that can be said in favour of the Rye House, except perhaps the fishing.'

But all this noisy fun came to an end and the Rye House decayed. Everything except the gatehouse disappeared. In 1950 Sir William Beech Thomas wrote that 'If there is any place in Hertfordshire which Hertfordshire ought to be a little ashamed of, it is Rye House, the building, not the place.' No one he questioned there even knew there was an actual building called the Rye House. When at last he found it:

> there was a repulsive ditch and some stagnant pools, but the more obvious way was blocked by nettles and timber that had fallen years ago. Finally by entering the ground through a tawdry painted wooden arch that announced a skating rink – a quite invisible skating rink – I made my way to within a few yards of the building, which might be a very picturesque ruin. There was once a well-kept garden almost up to the walls, of which the chief evidence was a number of straggling box-bushes that had once – or so I assumed – edged formal garden beds.

Two years later W. Branch Johnson also found the Rye House gatehouse 'little more than a ruin, roofless, dilapidated, and in part collapsed'. The lower floor, he noted, was now a Gents wc serving the roller-skating rink adjoining.

After learning the melodramatic history of the Rye House, and reading these depressing and relatively recent accounts, I set off half-expecting to find nothing at all. From Hoddesdon I drove down Rye Road, past Rye House railway station, crossed the Lea and saw the Rye House Hotel on the right – and on the left, standing in a neat patch of green field, with its bits of moat around it, the fifteenth-century gatehouse. There were also the old gateposts to the grounds – barley-sugar brick pillars, to match the single barley-sugar brick chimney on the gatehouse.

Inside, there was brick vaulting, and small rooms. I could not go upstairs because the whole structure was being restored and repaired. 'It's very old, isn't it?' I said to a workman. 'Yes,' he said. 'They say it's seventeenth-century.' (It's older than that.) He told me it was going to be opened as a little museum – it has probably been completed by now. The Rye House is being given a new lease of life as a staging post on walks in the Lea Valley Park – you can walk all the way from Ware to London, or spend an afternoon in one of the marshes, bird sanctuaries, nature reserves, boat-yards, sailing lakes, lidos, caravan parks, fishing places, country parks – and sewage works – along the way.

It's all a bit sanitized – a narrow strip of waterways, water-meadows and river valley transformed into a municipally approved playground. But it's better than Disneyland, and better by far than desolation and dereliction. The Rye House lives again. But who knows what someone writing about Hertfordshire will find in another hundred years?

Cussans, the nineteenth-century historian of Hertfordshire, was of the opinion that 'writing a County History is a sure sign of madness'. It certainly seems true in this county. Robert Clutterbuck, who published his history of Hertfordshire in 1817, was a brewer from Watford (there is a memorial to him in St Mary's Church there). He committed suicide by cutting his throat. Nathaniel Salmon was the curate at Westmill, but had to leave in 1695 when he refused to swear allegiance to Queen Anne. His history of Hertfordshire made no money and he starved to death in London.

The saddest case of all is that of Reginald Hine. He was born in 1883, in the village of Newnham – in the extremely beautiful moated house called Newnham Hall. When Herbert W. Tompkins visited Newnham in 1902 he referred to the pretty cottages of 'the peasants of Newnham', which is a little too feudal even for 1902, and to the fact that the village had no pub. (It still has no pub. This lack was originally due to the high principles of the then squire, Reginald Hine's father.) Mr Tompkins added that 'I can call to mind no names of man or woman who made this district famous by the accident of their birth.'

Reginald Hine was only nineteen at the time. For thirty-five years he worked as a solicitor in the firm of Hawkins & Co. in Portmill Lane in Hitchin, pursuing a lively second career as a local historian – which he was well placed to do, having access to the letters and records, the deeds and wills, of clients going back for generations, even before he started on the county archives and parish records. It was Hine, 'prince of Hertfordshire historians' as Sir William Beech Thomas calls him, who ploughed his way through three hundred pre-Reformation deeds to establish the origin of the ancient box trees in what had been my great-grandfather's garden.

Hine wrote over a dozen books about Hertfordshire, in his old-fashioned, cultivated, sometimes arch literary style. They included a *History of Hitchin* in two volumes, a book about notable and eccentric citizens called *Hitchin Worthies*, and an autobiography, *Confessions of an Uncommon Attorney*, which had great success with readers far beyond the county boundaries and brought him many friends.

It would seem to be an ideal life. He was a Hitchin Worthy himself, distinguished and charming, deeply involved in local affairs. He was married, and lived in a beautiful house, Willianbury. Willian is only just outside Letchworth Garden City but managed, as it still does, to retain its rural village identity.

Hine suffered from terrible depressions. There are hints of this, and of the tragedy to come, in his autobiography. He wrote that even as a young man there were times when 'I feared that my mind might crack at any moment. Everything seemed unreal and remote.' He read Freud on the interpretation of dreams, and threw the book on the fire. 'I loathed having read libidinous things that would be fixed in my memory for ever.' He himself had violent and extravagant dreams.

He wrote the last pages of his autobiography sitting in the ruins of St Nicholas's Church at Minsden, which is no longer a place exactly, but an area of scattered farms just north of Hitch Wood, less than a mile from Poynders End. The ruins are half-hidden in one of those wedges of woodland in the middle of fields, and linked to the narrow roads around by field-paths. It's usually called Minsden Chapel; as early as 1690 it was reported as being 'totally ruinated, stripped, uncovered, decayed, and demolished'. In 1701 Daniel Skingle, who had already been expelled from two Hertfordshire livings, was imprisoned at the instigation of Francis Bragge, vicar of Hitchin (and Sir Henry Chauncy's son-in-law) for preaching there.

But couples still chose to get married in this romantic place – during the last wedding, in July 1738, a piece of falling masonry knocked the book out of the curate's hand. A drawing of 1832 shows that there was still stone tracery in the windows then. Now, the crumbling flint walls are broken by irregular, eroded, empty spaces.

Reginald Hine, at the end of his autobiography, wrote that ruined Minsden was a place for those 'whose minds are in ruins'. He said he would like to die there, 'to sink down into this cool quietness of trees, to be softly surrounded with gleaming fantasies of foliage . . . .'

Minsden virtually belonged to Hine. He had leased it, for his lifetime, from the vicar of Hitchin. But he did not die there, as he had wished. On 14 April 1949, four years after writing the autobiography, he committed suicide at Hitchin Station by jumping in front of the 10.48 train from Cambridge. It was only going fifteen miles an hour, but he was killed. A friend, according to the local paper ('Hitchin Stunned by Mr R. L. Hine's Death'), said that just before the tragedy he and Hine had been sitting on a bench on the platform 'talking normally'. Hine left a note, which was not read out at the inquest.

He had retired from his legal practice two weeks before on his doctor's advice; he had just finished another book, about Charles Lamb and Hertfordshire, which was published posthumously. (It is not a very good book.) The doctor said that he had been treating Hine for thirteen years for 'threatened nervous breakdown'.[3]

He had bought a ticket for the 11.12 train to King's Cross. What did not come out at the inquest was that he was going up to London to appear before a disciplinary committee of the Law Society. He was acting in a divorce case, and had spoken not only with his client but with his client's spouse. This apparently is unprofessional behaviour, though it sounds like a sensible attempt at conciliation to me; the spouse's solicitor had lodged a complaint. It must have been the last straw for melancholic Reginald Hine.

Minsden Chapel on the edge of its little wood floats on fields of barley. In spring there are daffodils outside the ruined chancel. In summer, briony and deadly nightshade hang in the trees like lianas, and the nettles crowding the flint walls are shoulder-high.

Hine's ashes were scattered here. There is a stone in the ground at the entrance to the chapel, with his name, dates, and the words 'Historian of Hertfordshire' engraved on it. Some of the words have got worn away, or been erased, it's hard to tell which. He wrote of

Minsden that 'after my death and burial, I will endeavour, in all ghostly ways, to protect and haunt its hallowed walls'.

The saddest thing about Minsden is that there is no one here. There are not many Hertfordshire ghosts, and they are banal. The old inhabitants of Datchworth believe their lanes and cottages are haunted; a Grey Lady walks in Braughing, another Grey Lady walks in Watton-at-Stone, and a friar and five monks do eternal penance at Horse Cross (really 'Whore's Cross').

Anne Grimstone of Gorehambury lies in Tewin churchyard. She died in 1733 apparently declaring that she did not believe in the Resurrection, and that if there was life after death 'trees will render asunder my tomb'. Trees have rent asunder her tomb, quite violently. In the late nineteenth century, scores of people visited Tewin to marvel at this proof of life everlasting.

Tewin churchyard is elegiacally beautiful, with other spectacular tombs. These latter have as much to say about the generosity and prosperity of the inhabitants as their spirituality. The de Havillands of aeronautical fame lie here, and the Beits – diamond magnates, collectors of art, and friends of Cecil Rhodes, whose father was vicar of St Michael's at Bishop's Stortford. The Beits lived at Tewin Water, in grounds landscaped by Repton.

The manor at Markyate is called the Cell, being built on a former priory. The lady of the manor in the mid-seventeenth century, Kathleen Ferrers, led a double life; she was married at fourteen, and boredom drove her to crime. By night she was a highway robber, holding up travellers who passed through the village on Watling Street. One night she got shot, and crawled back to the Cell to die. The family covered up the embarrassing truth, and she was buried ceremoniously. But the Wicked Lady of Markyate Cell is said to ride out still, and local disasters are still ascribed to her influence.[4]

But Hertfordshire is not really a county for ghosts. Past and present crowd one another so closely here, in a ribbon development of linked lives, that the assertiveness of haunting seems unnecessary.

6

AUTHORS

Three of the women writers whose lives I have written had, by chance, some connection with Hertfordshire. Elizabeth Bowen's Aunt Laura kept house for her brother Wingfield Colley in Harpenden, which is still one of the nicest places in Hertfordshire – seemingly not sure whether it is a town or a village, but full of charm and confidence, with some very helpful natural advantages such as the wide and wavy common on its south-west side, and the river Lea forming a natural town boundary to the north-west.

Elizabeth Bowen's uncle was curate in charge of St John's. Elizabeth was thirteen when her mother died in September 1912; afterwards she lived with Aunt Laura and Uncle Wink at their house called South View in Harpenden, and was a day-pupil at Harpenden Hall – a partly sixteenth-century house set back on the east side of what Elizabeth called 'the airy, gold-gorsy Common' – before she went away to boarding-school. 'Breakfast', the first short story she ever completed, was written in the attic back bedroom of the Harpenden house.

Vita Sackville-West went to a ball at Hatfield House in January 1912; she and the young diplomat Harold Nicolson were staying in a house-party at The Grove, the Watford home of Lord Clarendon. Sometime after midnight, Vita and Harold were sitting on travelling-trunks on an upstairs landing at Hatfield, and he proposed to her. It turned out to be a highly unconventional marriage, but it lasted to the ends of their lives.

Rebecca West, a brilliant and newly famous young journalist, gave birth in 1914 to the illegitimate son of H. G. Wells. He was married, and had no intention of divorcing his wife. He found an isolated house for Rebecca and baby Anthony just outside Braughing, in the south-east of the county. The house was – and is – called Quinbury, and it stands down a farm-track leading from the hamlet of Hay Street, in the middle of cornfields, with the river Quin running nearby. Rebecca, who was twenty-two, was cut off from her friends and from professional contacts.

Quinbury is deeply rural now, in spite of being only thirty miles from London, and in 1914 it seemed the back of beyond. But Rebecca managed to keep up her journalism, made sporadic forays into London, and wrote her first book, a study of Henry James. Wells visited her when he could (and his legitimate son Frank, a film producer, was later to live at the Mill House at Digswell, on the Welwyn–Hertford road). But it was an unsatisfactory life for an ambitious and sociable girl, and Rebecca was often unhappy.

George Chapman, the Elizabethan translator of Homer, lived in Tilehouse Street, Hitchin. Sir Thomas More wrote his *Utopia* at Gobions, the family home at what is now Brookman's Park. William Cowper the poet (1731–1800) was born in the rectory (now rebuilt) at Berkhamsted.

Cowper is one of Hertfordshire's noble names. The family seat was at Panshanger, near Welwyn – a mansion built by William's kinsman the year the poet died. Local farmers were dispossessed of their land by compulsory purchase in order to surround the house in a big park landscaped by Humphry Repton, which included the already famous 'Panshanger Oak'.

William Cowper's serious poetry is not much read today, though churchgoers will know the hymns he wrote, 'Hark, my soul! It is the Lord', 'God moves in a mysterious way', and 'Oh, for closer walk with God'. Hertfordshire is strong in hymn-writers: the seventeenth-century Bishop Thomas Ken, a friend of Pepys and a famous preacher who attended Charles II in his last hours, was born at Little Berkhamsted (nothing to do with 'Great' Berkhamsted, which is miles away to the north-west). Ken wrote a morning hymn – 'Awake, my soul and with the sun/ Thy daily stage of duty run' – and an evening hymn, 'Glory to Thee, my God, this night'. The same famous verse, known as the Doxology, occurs in both:

> Praise God from whom all blessings flow,
> Praise Him all creatures here below;
> Praise Him above, ye heavenly host,
> Praise Father, Son, and Holy Ghost.

So far as Cowper is concerned, fewer people probably know his hymns than know his ebullient poem 'John Gilpin', about the mad gallop of the 'linen-draper bold' on a bolting horse from Cheapside straight through Edmonton on the Old North Road – where he was meant to be celebrating his twentieth wedding anniversary at The Bell – and thundering on, unable to stop the horse, to Ware:

> Said John – It is my wedding-day,
> And all the world would stare,
> If wife should dine at Edmonton
> And I should dine at Ware.

'John Gilpin' is a jolly ballad by the least jolly man imaginable. Cowper's mother, the rector's wife, died when he was six; there is a long memorial to her in St Peter's, Berkhamsted, which begins,

> Here lies, in early years bereft of life,
> The best of mothers and the kindest wife,

and ends,

> O stay a while, and shed a friendly tear,
> These lines, tho' weak, are as herself sincere.

Her son grew up with a melancholic temperament. His first school was in Markyate, run by a Dr Pitman, where he was bullied and utterly miserable. As a young man he had a nervous breakdown and was put into the care of Dr Nathaniel Cotton at his private asylum in St Albans, 'my little physician at St Albans' as Cowper referred to him. Love affairs, or the possibility of them, always brought on a crisis. He lived with and was most tenderly looked after by a Mrs Unwin, a vicar's widow. (Her husband, 'as he was riding one Sunday morning to his cure at Graveley, was thrown from his horse; of which fall he died.') When the question of Cowper's marrying nice Mrs Unwin came up, he had another breakdown, suffering from 'severe paroxysms of religious despondency', and tried to kill himself. This was not because he didn't like Mrs Unwin. 'My Mary', as he called her, was about the only person in the world he loved. But it was all just too much.

His first biographer, William Hayley, found mental illness hard to write about. In view of the candour of modern biography, Mr Hayley's agonized sensitivity is worth recording: 'The misfortune of mental derangement is a topic of such awful delicacy, that I consider it to be the duty of a biographer rather to sink, in tender silence, than to proclaim, with circumstantial and offensive temerity, the minute particulars of a calamity, to which all human beings are exposed . . .'[1]

Mrs Unwin took him back again. Cowper's Hertfordshire days were over, as she lived at Olney in Huntingdonshire. She seems to have provided for him not only a protective, accepting setting but a perpetual childhood. He kept a lot of pets – goldfinches, goldfish, hares, pigeons – about which he wrote his most sympathetic poems.

He wrote 'John Gilpin' in 1782; Mrs Unwin sent it to a newspaper and it was published anonymously. It became popular and famous when a comedian called Henderson got hold of it and incorporated it into his act. A couple of years later the ballad was included in Cowper's second published volume of poetry, and everyone was amazed to learn that he had written it. 'I'm not sorry that "John Gilpin", though hitherto he had been nobody's child, is likely to be owned at last,' wrote the author. 'I little thought, when I mounted him upon my Pegasus, that he would become so famous.'

Thanking a friend for the gift of a salmon, Cowper declared it had 'all the sweetness of a Hertfordshire trout, and resembles it so much in flavour, that blindfold I should not have known the difference'. Izaak Walton's *Compleat Angler,* in which Hertfordshire trout play no small part, was already an old and famous book in Cowper's lifetime. It was published in the 1650s. Walton, a linen-draper from Stafford who was a friend of John Donne and of many great men of his time, lived from 1593 to 1683. His wife Ann was a Hertfordshire girl, being the half-sister of the saintly Bishop Ken.

Izaak Walton fished the Lea river from Waltham Cross to Ware, taking in Hoddesdon and lovely Great Amwell. He knew the Lea Valley backwards, and it was all lovely then, once you escaped the horse-drawn traffic of the Old North Road. The Thatched House at Hoddesdon, one of his favourite drinking places, has gone; but he probably drank too in The Fish and Eels, which you will find by winding past Dobb's Weir and its pool, past the geese in the water-meadows, over a little bridge and (just for a moment) into Essex, on the eastern bank of the Lea.

Angling, wrote Izaak Walton, 'is an art, and an art worthy the knowledge and practice of a wise man'. Here is his description of how to prepare a frog for bait, just to give a flavour of his knowledge, his practice and his art:

> Put your hook, I mean the arming-wire, through his mouth, and out at his gills; and then with a fine needle and silk sew the upper part of his leg, with only one stitch, to the arming-wire of your hook; or tie the frog's leg, above the upper joint, to the armed-wire; and, in so doing, use him as though you loved him.

The *Compleat Angler* begins with praise of the waters and the watering-holes of the Lea Valley. 'All lovers of Hertfordshire should know the first chapter of the *Compleat Angler* almost by heart.'[2] I don't suppose there are many that do, today. The man who wrote that also wrote: 'It has been said that there are just two English authors for whom the public feel not so much admiration as affection. They are established as friends. The two are Izaak Walton and Charles Lamb; and both had a peculiar over-riding delight in Hertfordshire.'

But who reads Charles Lamb now? *Tales from Shakespeare*, designed to make the stories of the plays accessible to children, and which he wrote in collaboration with his sister Mary, may still be found on library shelves. Lamb wrote some enduring lines of poetry: 'All, all are gone, the old familiar faces.' It would seem incredible, to anyone with traditional literary tastes at the turn of the century, that he should be so forgotten. But the modernists, and two World Wars, put him out of fashion.

Lamb is, or was, most famous for his essays, like Francis Bacon, and the essay is a neglected, forgotten form; Lamb's essays are whimsical, mannered, amusing, perceptive, 'civilized'. Schoolchildren keen to please their teachers, and the writers of third leaders in *The Times*, modelled their style on his. Occasionally he used a word which does not fit this image – as when, writing in an essay called 'A Quakers' Meeting' about possession by the spirit, he referred to 'the old Foxian orgasm'. The *Oxford English Dictionary* cites the sexual meaning of 'orgasm' from the seventeenth century, and notes its use in the eighteenth century to signify any kind of paroxysm – of rage, violence, or strong feeling. Possibly it was so unthinkable to use 'orgasm' in print in a sexual sense in Lamb's kind of writing that his usage was, paradoxically, perfectly proper.

The facts of Lamb's life are tragic enough. He was born in 1775, and at the age of seventeen got a job as a clerk to the East India Company, where he remained until he retired. He had a breakdown in his youth; his sister Mary had more severe fits of insanity, and in one of these she killed their mother with a knife. Lamb took charge of his sister and devoted much of his life to looking after her.

He was at school in Hertford with Samuel Taylor Coleridge ('Coleridge holds that a man cannot have a pure mind who refuses apple-dumplings. I am not certain but that he is right.'), and was the friend of Wordsworth, Southey and other literary men; he was intensely convivial and much loved by his friends. He was a tiny little man, and an indefatigable talker and walker. He smoked too much and drank dangerously. Cantankerous Thomas Carlyle had no time for Lamb, and left a most unflattering picture of him:

> Charles Lamb, I sincerely believe to be in some considerable degree *insane*. A more pitiful, ricketty, grasping, staggering, stammering Tom fool I do not know. He is witty by denying truisms, and abjuring good manners. His speech wriggles hither and thither with an incessant painful fluctuation; not an opinion in it or a fact or even a phrase that you can thank him for ... Besides he is now a confirmed shameless drunkard; *asks* vehemently for gin-and-water in strangers' houses; tipples till he is utterly mad, and is only not thrown out of doors because he is too much despised for taking such trouble with him. Poor Lamb! Poor England where such a despicable abortion was named genius![3]

Carlyle did not at this time know the Lambs' awful family history, but it would not have made much difference. And the point is that the 'ricketty little tippler' was considered a genius by lots of people, both in his own time and afterwards.

Lamb published his essays in the *London Magazine* in the early 1820s, and they came out in book form as the *Essays of Elia*. He wrote of 'Slow journeying on/ To the green plains of Hertfordshire' in a sonnet, but it was in the essays that his love of the county – 'hearty, homely, loving Hertfordshire' – was chiefly expressed.

Lamb was a Londoner – a Cockney, as Carlyle chose to put it. Hertfordshire was his Paradise Lost and his Promised Land. His grandmother Mary Field was housekeeper to the Plumer family at a house called Blakesware Manor, across the little river Ash north of the road between Wareside and Widford. He used to stay with his grandmother as a child, and go round the big house with her as she went about her work, entranced by the tapestries and pictures. The old house was pulled down in Lamb's lifetime (the present mansion is Victorian), and the essay he wrote about it was provoked by his discovery of its ruins. 'Why, every plank and panel of that house for me had magic in it.' Nearby in a cottage called Blenheims (now demolished) lived Ann Simmons, whom he courted 'for seven long years, in hope sometimes, sometimes in despair' – until she married someone else. His essay 'Dream Children' is about the children she and he never had.

The other place he loved was Mackery or Mackerye End, to the west, just north-east of the Harpenden–Wheathampstead road. (It's not easy to find. Take the turn off the main road at Batford Mill, opposite the Cherry Tree Inn.) His great-aunt Gladman, his grandmother's sister, lived at the farm. 'The oldest thing I remember is Mackery End, or Mackarel End, as it is spelt, perhaps more properly, in some old maps of Hertfordshire ... I can just remember having been taken there, on a visit to a great-aunt, under the care of Bridget' – who was an older cousin. Forty years on, he returned there with the same cousin, and made the acquaintance of unknown relations. 'Those slender ties, that prove slight as gossamer in the rending atmosphere of a metropolis, bind faster, as we found it, in hearty, homely, loving Hertfordshire.'

The farm is still there, and the glorious seventeenth-century manor house of Mackerye End of which the farm would have been a dependency. The hamlet was 'quite a place of pilgrimage' when Herbert W. Tompkins was there in 1902. 'Good literary Americans return to their country shamefaced if they have not visited Lamb's Mackery End.'

Lamb's sentimental affection for Hertfordshire was put to the test when in 1812 he inherited a dream cottage here from his godfather, an oil-merchant of Holborn in London. The cottage was – and is – called Button Snap, and it is a little, ground-hugging, thatched thing, standing on its own, on an unmetalled track from Cherry Green, south-west of Westmill. It is lonely enough now; before modern transport, it was punitively so, a dwelling for a hermit. The track leads on to Wakeley Farm, all that remains of a deserted medieval village.

The first thing you see as you approach Button Snap on foot is not the cottage itself, which is set back, but something odd that seems to have been dumped on the grassy verge beside it. It turns out to be a large brownish marble plaque set in the bank, with a relief carving of Charles Lamb's head in white marble within it. It was brought here by the Charles Lamb Society from a demolished building in London. It could not have been hung on the cottage; it would be quite out of scale. It is a large, urban, sophisticated piece, and it looks pathetic and incongruous lying there in the grass. There is emerald lichen in Lamb's marble eye-sockets, and in the folds of his bow-cravat.

Lamb only kept the cottage for three years; then he sold it, for £15. 'I had thought', he wrote in 1822, 'to have retired to Ponders End, emblematic name, how beautiful! in the Ware road – toddling about it and Cheshunt, anon stretching on some fine Izaak Walton morning, to Hoddesdon or Amwell, careless as a beggar; but walking, walking ever, till I fairly walked myself off my legs, dying walking.' He died, in 1834, at Edmonton, at the London end of the Ware road. 'All, all are gone, the old familiar faces.'

A distressing number of the writers who were associated with Hertfordshire in earlier centuries turn out to have been mad or melancholy, and not so much obscure as obscured, by changing literary tastes. Another melancholy Hertfordshire writer, and the founder of 'the graveyard school of poetry' of which Gray's 'Elegy' is a more durable example, was Edward Young. Having failed in his first ambitions and being well into middle age, he took orders and became rector of

Welwyn and lord of the manor there in 1730. He was a discontented, painfully shy and painfully ambitious man; when he preached at court, it seemed to him that the lordly congregation was not listening to him, and he burst into tears.

Welwyn was then a village, making its living by servicing travellers along the Great North Road. Its coaching inns were famous. Pepys often stayed in the town on his way through Hertfordshire; it was the stop after Stevenage. In 1661 he and his wife had a bed each at the inn, 'and so lay single, and still remember it that of all the nights I ever slept in my life I never did pass a night with more epicureanism of sleep ... I never had so much content in all my life, and so my wife says it was with her.'

Old Welwyn is still an attractive place, bypassed now by arterial roads, and working very hard and successfully to be itself and not just a tasteful appendage of Welwyn Garden City. A completely forgotten poet, Theodore Hook (1788–1841) wrote the following lines about the place:

> You ask me where in peaceful grot
>   I'd like to fix my dwelling?
> I'll tell you, for I've found the spot;
>   And mortals call it Welwyn.
> Its shade a solitude imparts
>   All other shades excelling;
> The county where it stands is Herts.
>   And hearts are lost in Welwyn.[4]

For some reason, Samuel Taylor Coleridge thought this man was a genius.

In Welwyn's Mill Lane, which runs down to a little bridge over the Mimram, with a beautiful mill-house and some very desirable waterside cottages, we trespassed in the garden of a particularly good-looking timbered house. When challenged I apologized humbly, as I always do at these embarrassing moments, and explained that I was writing a book about Hertfordshire. 'Oh, are you? I've written one,' said the owner of this formerly moated medieval manor house. Within five minutes he had sold me a copy.[5] He was Tony Rook, author, archaeologist and founding editor of the *Hertfordshire Archaeological*

Review. The Welwyn Archaeological Society, also founded by Tony Rook, displays Roman pots and Saxon skulls in a shop-window opposite the church where Edward Young took the services.

Young's wife and her two children by a previous marriage all died within a short time. When his step-daughter was very ill with consumption, Young took her to the south of France. She died while they were there, and the story is that because she was a Protestant the local priest denied her Christian burial; poor old Young, with the help of a servant, had to dig a hole in a field and bury her himself. It's just the sort of thing that would happen to him, but it's only a story. The records show that the step-daughter was properly buried in the Protestant cemetery at Lyons.[6]

It was after this that Young came home to Welwyn and wrote his gloomy meditation in blank verse, *The Complaint: Night Thoughts on Life, Death and Immortality* (1742), generally known as *Night Thoughts*. It was greatly to the taste of his times, and was translated into German and French, in which languages it was much admired. Young was never cheerful exactly, but he moved from the rectory into Guessens, a fine house still standing, laid down a bowling-green, and built the Assembly Rooms as part of his effort to turn Welwyn into a fashionable spa. There are chalybeate springs here, as there are also at Cuffley and Barnet, which were also exploited as spas. At the Barnet Wells, Pepys in 1664 'drank three glasses, and walked and came back and drank three more'. When he got home, 'not being very well, I betimes to bed'.

Maybe the effects of Hertfordshire waters on the system were rather violent, though Chauncy wrote of them that 'they purge very kindly, dissolve acid, tough Phlegm in the Stomach and Guts and are of great efficiency in cholicks'. Pepys tended to put a strain on his digestion. After taking three glasses of the Barnet waters on another occasion, he went to the Red Lion, 'and there drank, and eat some of the best cheese-cakes that I ever eat in my life'. He went on to Hatfield where he and his companion stopped at the inn 'next my Lord Salisbury's house, and there rested ourselves, and drank and bespoke dinner'.

Apropos of the Red Lion in Barnet, it seems a pointless 'improvement', in view of its long tradition, that its prominent sign – a rampant red lion standing out above the road, and a local landmark –

should recently have been gilded, and the place renamed the Dandy Lion. (Barnet is since 1965 part of Greater London, but history places it in Hertfordshire.)

Jane Austen set *Pride and Prejudice* in Hertfordshire, though there is no evidence that she ever spent time here. When silly Lydia Bennet runs away with Mr Wickham, they search for her all along the Great North Road between Barnet and Hatfield. Saturnine Mr Darcy, who takes a house near the Bennets, is 'not at all liked in Hertfordshire'. The fictional town 'Meryton' is probably Hertford, and people speculate that the Bennets' village, one mile out, is Hertingfordbury – but no one can be sure (least of all, I suspect, Miss Austen).

Charles Dickens's Hertfordshire is less notional. His first known visit was in 1835 as a young man of twenty-three, when he came to Hatfield to report for the *Morning Chronicle* the dreadful fire at Hatfield House in which the dowager first Marchioness of Salisbury, a keen rider to hounds in spite of her advanced age, was burned to death. She had started the fire by overturning a candle in her room.

In *Oliver Twist*, it is at Barnet that Oliver is picked up by the Artful Dodger, who takes him into London and to Fagin. After Bill Sikes murders Nancy in the same novel, he flees from London and ends up in a small pub at the foot of Fore Street in Hatfield, where the bloodstains on his hat attract attention. This pub is believed to be the Eight Bells, which bears a plaque announcing the distinction.

Dickens also made Hatfield the setting for two short stories about a Mrs Lirriper, who keeps a lodging house in Norfolk Street. Bleak House, which gives its name to my favourite novel by Dickens, is at the top of a hill – perhaps Gombards Road or Catherine Street – just outside St Albans, and it was not bleak at all but a 'quite delightful place'.

Dickens often stayed at Knebworth House, as the guest of his friend the poet, politician and novelist Bulwer-Lytton, author of *The Last Days of Pompeii* – which I cite because it is the only book of his I have ever read. Visitors to Knebworth can see the playbills for the amateur dramatics that were performed there, in which Dickens was a moving spirit. He and Bulwer-Lytton used the ticket-money to fund their Guild of Literature and Art, which was to provide support for writers and artists who had fallen on evil days. Some ornate villas in Stevenage were built to provide homes for poverty-stricken artists of all kinds, but the scheme was a failure. No one wanted to live in the houses. They were sold off in 1897 and are now demolished, as is the original pub called Our Mutual Friend, named after one of Dickens's novels, though a modern pub in the New Town has been given the same name.

Another Victorian novelist, Anthony Trollope, lived in Hertfordshire from 1859 to 1871. His mother had lived for the first months of her widowhood at a house on Hadley Common while Trollope was a junior clerk at the London Post Office, and part of *The Bertrams* is set in Hadley. His sister Emily is buried in the church there. Trollope and his wife rented and subsequently bought Waltham House at Waltham Cross – a large and pretty house behind ornamental gates, which is no longer there, though after the Trollopes left it was lived in by the Pauls, of the famous rose-growing family. The Trollopes kept cows and pigs, grew vegetables, and were proud of their strawberries. Trollope, who loved hunting, rode to hounds over the border in Essex.

It was while Trollope was at Waltham House that he gave up his job to devote himself entirely to writing books. One of his sons had emigrated to Australia, and it was when they went to visit him there that the decision was taken to give up the Hertfordshire house. It remained on the market for some time and was in the end sold at a loss. Trollope was a good businessman and made a lot of money out of his writing. He bewailed in his autobiography that, while he was always hearing of other people making a profit out of selling property, he did not seem to be lucky that way himself. 'I presume I am not well adapted for transactions of that kind.'

The most important twentieth-century author to have made Hertfordshire his home was George Bernard Shaw. His house at Ayot St Lawrence was originally built as the rectory. He and his wife Charlotte rented it from 1906, when it was only a few years old, and bought it outright after the First World War. What decided Shaw to take the rectory was a tombstone inscription in the churchyard, a memorial to Mary Anne South who had lived to be seventy: 'Her Time Was Short'. Shaw's time was not short, even by Ayot standards. He died there in 1950, aged ninety-four. His ashes, and Charlotte's, were sprinkled in the garden.

The heroine of one of Shaw's plays, *Village Wooing*, was based on the village postmistress, Mrs Jisbella Lyth. Shaw hardly ever went into the post office himself; he would send a hand-delivered letter with his requests for stamps. But when he heard that Mrs Lyth was ill, he sent his car and chauffeur to take her to hospital.

Shaw was not the only unusual inhabitant this small village has known. Sir Lionel Lyde, a late-eighteenth-century lord of the manor who had made his fortune in tobacco, built the new Palladian parish church in the style of the Temple of Apollo at Delos, reducing the old twelfth-century church to a picturesque ruin. King Michael of Romania lived at Ayot House during the Second World War. (Later Ayot House became a silk farm, where the material for robes and christening gowns for the royal family was woven.)

Shaw's Hertfordshire life was 'a living advertisement for his vegetarianism, teetotalism, economic philosophy and hygienic clothing'.[7] His house, which was first called Shaw's Corner by the village people, is an austere and rather unattractive monument to these values, both outside and in. Neither Shaw nor his wife seems to have had any aesthetic sense at all when it came to interior decoration.

The visitor has access to the downstairs, and to the garden. The Shaws had a lovely view. At the bottom of the garden is the 'summerhouse' – a shed – in which Shaw used to escape from the house and work in peace. In this simple, cramped little space is a desk, a telephone, a day-bed. It looks as if he might come back at any moment. And in spite of the plainness and even the ugliness of the house and its furnishings, it is exciting and moving to see Shaw's study with all his belongings arranged more or less as he left them.

One should not ascribe the number of portraits and busts of the great man purely to his narcissism; he had arranged with the National Trust that the house should be taken over after his death, and memorabilia were collected with this in mind. James Lees-Milne visited the house on behalf of the Trust in 1944; he lunched in Hitchin at a 'British Restaurant' (cheap wartime eating-places set up in all towns) and went on to Shaw's Corner, which he described gloomily in his diary as 'a very ugly, dark red-brick villa, built in 1902'.[8] Nevertheless the Trust agreed to take it on. Shaw died in 1950; the following year, Shaw's Corner was opened to the public by Dame Edith Evans.

Shaw adored many of the actresses who appeared in his plays, among them the great Ellen Terry. Nearly forty years before Shaw established himself in Hertfordshire, Ellen Terry spent half a dozen years off-stage in retirement at Fallows Green, now part of Harpenden. At the age of twenty-one she was already a famous actress, separated from the painter George Frederic Watts (whom she had married when she was sixteen and he was forty-seven), when she fell in love with the architect Edward William Godwin, who built the house at Harpenden in which they lived.

To start with, it was a romantic idyll: 'I have the simplest faith that absolute devotion to another human being means the greatest happiness. That happiness was now mine.' At the Harpenden house Ellen Terry reared her two children by Godwin, one of whom became the artist, actor and stage-designer Gordon Craig. (He was actually born in Orchard Road, Stevenage, and the theatre which forms part of New Stevenage's leisure centre is named after him.) She also kept two hundred ducks and chickens, and did her own cooking and washing with the help of one little servant.

There was happiness, but no money. One day in 1874 Ellen was driving down a narrow lane when the wheel of her pony-cart fell off. While she stood there wondering what to do next, a whole crowd of horsemen in pink coats came leaping over the hedge into the lane.

> One of them stopped and asked if he could do anything. Then he looked hard at me and exclaimed:
> 'Good God! It's Nelly!'
> The man was Charles Reade.
> 'Where have you been all these years?' he said.
> 'I have been having a very happy time,' I answered.
> 'Well, you've had it long enough. Come back to the stage!'
> 'No, never!'
> Suddenly I remembered the bailiff in the house a few miles away, and I said laughingly: 'Well, perhaps I would think of it if someone would give me forty pounds a week!'[9]

Her old friend Charles Reade was a novelist, a playwright and a theatrical manager. Ellen Terry went back to London. It meant the end of her liaison with the father of her children. She made two more disastrous marriages, but enjoyed a long and triumphant partnership with the great Henry Irving on the London stage and, in her maturity, became 'sweetheart–mother' to George Bernard Shaw.

The grandparents of Beatrix Potter, author of the Peter Rabbit books, retired to Camfield Place near Essendon, where Beatrix often used to stay with them. Camfield has wonderful grounds, a grotto, a mammoth oak tree planted by Elizabeth I, farmland and woodlands, and wide uninterrupted views. Beatrix Potter's grandfather remodelled the old house in the 1860s, but the walled garden is part of the original building; the bricks are Elizabethan. Many of the little animals and birds, as well as the beds, chairs and small household objects such as candlesticks in Beatrix Potter's illustrations for her little books were copied from those she knew at Camfield.

Another Hertfordshire house close by that Beatrix Potter knew well was Bedwell Lodge, where she spent a summer with her parents; Bedwell Park was the home of the philanthropic brewer Samuel Whitbread. She used the potting-shed and geraniums at Bedwell in her illustrations for the story of Peter Rabbit. Tradition has it that the walled garden at Camfield was the scene for Peter Rabbit's encounter with Mr McGregor, but the illustrations show that this cannot be right; Mr McGregor's garden is bounded by a hedge. But the gate under which Peter could not squeeze is at Camfield.

The present owner of Camfield Place is the prolific romantic novelist Barbara Cartland, who has lived there since 1950. She takes an energetic interest in local affairs, having been a county councillor for nine years; she has been a campaigner for Hertfordshire gypsies, and instrumental in changing the law so that local authorities are now obliged to allocate sites for gypsy camps. Not that this is always done with good grace: in our own village, there was a meeting in the village hall to protest against the allocation of a site on our boundaries. The objection to gypsies seemed to be twofold and contradictory: first, that they were so poor and dirty that they would be thieving round the village and their children would bring lice into the school; secondly (and conversely), that they were so well-off and prosperous, with expensive cars, and all mod cons provided by the taxpayer, that they didn't need any help from anyone.

Barbara Cartland felt otherwise. In 1964 she established her own

Romany camp on her own land, which the gypsies, she says, called 'Barbaraville'. And at Camfield Place she plants geraniums, since they are, she says, the only flowers which Peter Rabbit's friends and relations do not eat.

Stevie Smith the poet and novelist would have trespassed on the Camfield estate in the early 1930s, when it belonged to Lord Queenborough. She lived with her aunt in Palmers Green in north London, and this part of Hertfordshire was her playground, for long weekend walks and sexual adventures which tended to end sadly.

Stevie came out to Hertford North by train with her German friend Karl on a wet day, as she tells in her autobiographical *Novel on Yellow Paper* (1936), and on their walk they came across a big empty house in a wood; Stevie, being thin and agile, broke in through the pantry window. 'There was inside a musty fusty smell suggesting murder, suicide and avarice. We found some sacking, and it was damned cold in there, and we lay down there in each other's arms . . .'

The deserted house reminded Stevie Smith of houses in the books of Mrs Humphry Ward, a late-Victorian novelist – specializing in social and religious themes – famous in her own time; she too lived in Hertfordshire, in the house called Stocks (later a girls' school) at Aldbury, nestling under the great woods of Ashridge in the north-west of the county. Aldous Huxley, one of Mrs Humphry Ward's nephews, said that she 'rolled off her plots like sections of macadamized road'. One of these, set in Aldbury, was *The Story of Bessie Costrell*, which she dashed off in fifteen days.

Stevie Smith brought another young man to Hertfordshire, suburban Freddy from Palmers Green (to whom she was briefly engaged), and there was, after a rift and a reconciliation, 'all of that Hertfordshire excursion to do again, the pubs and teashops to visit, the churchyards to explore, the hedgerows to sit beside, with all of the deep dark impenetrable forest for our playground'. There was 'all of the lovely countryside of Hertfordshire for our walks together':

Now I suspect that for me Hertfordshire is the operative word, and you have yourself no doubt already suspected this for a long time. Oh lovely Hertfordshire, so quiet and unassuming, so much of the real countryside, so little of beastly over-rated bungaloid Surrey–Sussex with all of its uproar of weekend traffic to and from Bloomsbury, Hertfordshire is my love and always has been, it is so unexciting, so quiet, its woods so thick and abominably drained, so pashy underneath, if you do not know the lie of the land you had better keep out. Yes, I think anyway, you had better keep out. You can run for miles in Monk's Green Woods and never see a soul, and you can lie in the bracken and watch the bailiff go by and wish his gun would go off on him.[10]

But 'darling little Freddy' grew sick of Hertfordshire. Stevie Smith did not, though in the end she grew sick of Freddy.

7

GODLINESS

ertfordshire was the birthplace of the only English pope
there has ever been, Nicholas Breakspear. He was born
around 1100 at Bedmond, a hamlet near King's Langley.
His father became a monk at St Alban's, where the boy
was not welcome. He went off to Europe; and returned to St Alban's
just once, a local hero, as Pope Adrian IV. He died in 1159 and is
buried in St Peter's in Rome.

St Thomas à Becket, when he was Chancellor, lived in state at
Berkhamsted Castle; his first living as a young priest was at Bramfield.
The great family home of St Thomas More, another obstinate martyr
to the greater obstinacy of monarchy, was Gobions, near what is now
Brookman's Park. The family held on to it after More's execution until
1702. In 1836 it was pulled down by the owner of a seventeenth-
century house called Brookmans, to add the grounds to his own estate.
Brookmans itself was destroyed by fire in 1891, and the whole area,
just north of Potters Bar, is now prosperous, leafy commuterland.
Thomas More would not recognize it. But the name Gobions survives
in the woods and public parkland to the south, and a castellated 'folly
arch', erected off Hawkshead Lane by a later owner of old Gobions,
still stands.

The typical Hertfordshire church is topped by a squat tower from
which rises a narrow spire of wood covered with lead – the 'Hert-

fordshire spike', a landmark leading the traveller from one village or town to the next. The clean, polished, flower-filled, often whitewashed and usually empty interiors of most of Hertfordshire's churches would seem extraordinary to our ancestors. In 1581, in the reign of Elizabeth I, church attendance was made compulsory by law, with heavy fines for shirkers. Religion was politics, then. It is a paradox that at a time when country congregations are a fraction of what they were even a hundred years ago, the churches themselves are more hospitable and in a better state of repair than they have been since they were new-built – in spite or because of the endless fund-raising appeals, and not counting those churches that have been abandoned to the nettles and the owls.

Even the churches that never fell into disuse were, before the Reformation and at various stages after, in an indescribable state of filth and disrepair. As we have seen, local people made off with any loose material to repair their own houses with. Animals wandered in and out, windows were broken, there were often no vestments or vessels, and the clergy were frequently absentees: at Graveley, a couple got married, or married themselves, *de verbo*.

The sixteenth and seventeenth centuries, which saw violent changes of regimes and established religion, seem like a dire musical comedy so far as parish churches are concerned. When the monarch was Protestant, churchwardens sold off the Catholic ceremonial gear; when the monarch was Roman Catholic, everything had to go back as before, and married priests were deprived of their livings. Whichever branch of the Christian Church was in power, someone somewhere was being burned for heresy. Apparently petty ritualistic disagreements ruined and sometimes cost lives. The Revd Charles Chauncy's trouble at Ware, which caused his emigration to America, was because Archbishop Laud decreed that Communion-tables should be in the chancel, and protected by rails from wandering dogs and other godless goings on in the body of the church; though any self-respecting dog, one would imagine, would be able to leap over your average altar rail. There were similar rows over altar rails, and over stained-glass windows, at Much Hadham.

But Hertfordshire seems to have accepted the consequences of the Reformation, and all the succeeding swings and roundabouts, with

The Eight Bells at Hatfield

Rook's Nest, Stevenage: E. M. Forster's Howards End

George Orwell's cottage at Wallington

Charles Lamb in marble, on the grass at Button Snap

Ruins of Minsden Chapel: 'for those whose minds are in ruins'

G. B. Shaw's summerhouse at Ayot St Lawrence

Lombard House in Hertford, where Chauncy wrote his History

Trees bursting through Lady Anne Grimston's tomb at Tewin

St Alban's Cathedral

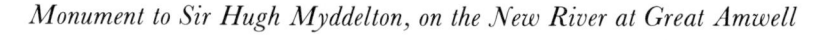

Disused church beside the farmyard at Caldecote

Monument to Sir Hugh Myddelton, on the New River at Great Amwell

Abandoned church at Thundridge: the village moved away

characteristic phlegm. During the Civil War, three thousand Par-
liamentary soldiers were quartered at Hitchin. They did a great deal
of damage to the church. Those who remained loyal to the Stuarts
suffered for it. Among these were the lords of Furneux Pelham Hall,
a great early-Elizabethan house which was ransacked, robbed and
sequestered as a punishment. Later the family got it back; today, deer
graze in the meadow on one side of the narrow lane that passes the
house (and are sold as venison on the other). On the forecourt of the
great house a peacock poses, and a King Charles spaniel barks at the
passer-by. On certain weekends in the summer, the gardens are open
to the public.

Arthur, Lord Capel, of Little Hadham Hall raised a troop for the
king – unsuccessfully. He was sent to the Tower, escaped, but was
finally beheaded. His heart was put in a box in the muniment room
of his house; at the Restoration, it was presented to Charles II as a
memento. (It's hard to know what one would do with a present like
that.)

Another of those who suffered for supporting Charles I was William
Clerke of Chesfield. On 28 April 1645, when Henry Chauncy was
still a schoolboy at the grammar school in Bishop's Stortford, three
strangers in that town asked the way to Graveley. They were later
seen near Tewin on the banks of the river Mimram, near a footbridge;
if that is true, they were going to Graveley by a most roundabout way,
in a south-westerly loop. The rumour was that one of the three was
the doomed Charles I in disguise, on his way – again by an extremely
circuitous route – to join the Scots at Newark.

If King Charles was going to Graveley, he was probably making
for Chesfield Park up the hill, William Clerke's house. But if my
calculations are correct, William Clerke had already been dead ten
months; perhaps the king was coming to see the family. In her introduction to the 1975 reissue of Chauncy's history, Carola Oman wrote
that the 'wildly romantic' story of Charles's journey through Hertfordshire in disguise 'was still current in Tewin Lower Green Women's
Institute in the 1920s'. That's maybe a nice way of saying that she
didn't believe a word of it.

It's also said that Charles I was later brought through Baldock as a
prisoner, in the charge of Fairfax, and that the rector brought him

out some wine from the church in the chalice; and that the Princess Anne, daughter of James II and later queen, fled the court at the approach of trouble and slept a night in Hitchin, in the street called Bancroft, in late 1688. Her contact there was William Bromfield (who married the daughter of the lord of the manor of Chesfield), spy and adviser to James II. Bromfield was a chancer who did time both in the Bastille and in Newgate. He was an apothecary – a profession which seemed to cover a multitude of meddlings. Pockets of Roman Catholicism survived strongly after the fall of James II – in Standon, for example, and Bishop's Stortford, both in the east of the county.

Hertfordshire has a history of peculiar clergymen. My least favourite is Francis Bragge, who was vicar of Hitchin from 1690 until 1715, when he went into retirement at Great Wymondeley. There is a black marble slab to him in Hitchin Church, where he is described as a labourer in Christ's vineyard. He married Jane, Sir Henry Chauncy's daughter. Only five feet high, he was a sadistic little person. He made 'sinners', i.e. people he disapproved of, stand for hours in the chancel of Hitchin Church draped in white sheets, doing penance. He was an alcoholic, and built a brew-house for his own private use before and after services at the south gate of the church. He was also prominent in persecuting a so-called witch, and making money out of the case afterwards, as we shall see presently.

The list of incumbents in Rushden Church announces that in the sixteenth century, with 'the chancel in disrepair', the vicar was dismissed. Neglect of parish duties was but the mildest of clerical eccentricities. The Revd William Jones, curate and then vicar of Broxbourne from 1781 to 1821, had a coffin made to measure for himself. He stood the coffin up on end in his study and had it fitted with bookshelves. About twelve years later, feeling himself to be near death, he had the books and the shelves taken out, and duly died. But he had put on weight in the interim, and was only squeezed into it with embarrassing indignity.

The Revd Ogle Russell Lafont, vicar of Hinxworth in the midnineteenth century, tried to force his way into 10 Downing Street during a Cabinet meeting, insisting he was the Prime Minister. Drink was often the problem – as in the case of the Revd John Henry Butt of the parish of Layston with Buntingford, who in 1882 was accused by his bishop of persistent drunkenness, frequenting taverns and ale-houses, and using indecent language in public. These last instances were noted by the historian Cussans, whose descriptions of the interiors of churches in the first decades of Victoria's reign modify one's view of what are now thought of as 'Victorian values'. If they are what they are meant to be, they are very *late* Victorian values.

He describes how the Cockenhatch pew in Barkway Church was, until it was taken down in 1862, 'a jolly pew', like a room, with windows and a fireplace inside. It belonged to the Clinton family of Cockenhatch or Cokenach, the moated house north-east of Barkway on the Cambridge road. Once inside their private pew, the occupants 'were not obliged to listen to the service, nor, as I am told, did they often do so'. They shut the windows, pulled down the blinds, drew their chairs round the fire, smoked their pipes and chatted away till the service was over.

The isolated thirteenth-century parish church of Flaunden, on the Buckinghamshire border, was squatted in by poor families and their hens in the nineteenth century. Cussans had painful experience of the neglect into which many Hertfordshire churches had fallen in the 1870s. He found Offley Church thick with dust and cobwebs, unswept for years. When he rolled up the matting in the chancel to look at the inscriptions on the floor he found not only an inch of dust, but fleas. He was wearing lavender-coloured trousers; he rushed into the vestry, took off his trousers, shook out 'some thousands' of fleas, and finished his researches 'in the costume of Adam before the Fall … How I afterwards went into a bedroom at the Sun in Hitchin, under the specious pretence of washing my hands, and left a legacy of some fifty Offley fleas for the next unhappy traveller, I need not enlarge on.'[1] It used to be fashionable to deplore and to sneer at the great wave of church restoration and redecoration that began in the late nineteenth century; but if it had not happened, the village churches of England would now be in a state of filthy, crumbling dereliction.

Reginald Hine devoted a chapter of his *Hitchin Worthies* to 'A Group of Eccentrics', prominent among whom is yet another man of God, the Revd John Alington (1795–1863). Letchworth, in his day, was a small village. Alington inherited the lordship of the manor, and came to live at Letchworth Hall. He proceeded to take over the church services from the rector, leaving him with nothing to do but bury the dead. Alington invented the services as he went along, and preached free love from the pulpit.

When the bishop put a stop to this, Alington took to conducting services at home. He kept open house, with a special welcome for gypsies, tramps, and 'all the whores of Hertfordshire'. On a two-wheeled hobby-horse he careered up and down the hall, 'cheering wildly as he rebounded from the brick wall at one end and the wooden screen at the other. If he fell off, which happened every other turn, he would roar with laughter, and bow to the congregation before he remounted the machine.'

He preached thunderous sermons, draped in a leopard skin; and after divine service there was always a party, with dancing and sex. (Hine does not put it that way, but it's what he means.) There was cockfighting in the garden. Sometimes Alington put on his leopard skin at night and went out to frighten the people of Hitchin or Baldock. He was mad, by any reckoning. But he was a genuine democrat and a practical if unorthodox Christian (unlike his holier-than-thou neighbours), constantly instructing and exhorting the estate workers and vagrants who were his only real friends; he read Shakespeare to them while they soaked up his ale; he could also sew, paint, and play musical instruments.

Late in life he married a girl from the village, an attractive, illiterate slip of a thing called Elizabeth Tuffnell. The gentry declined his invitations to the wedding, so he called in the poor from the fields around. In the 1840s, after this marriage, he undertook ambitious building works at Letchworth Hall, adding a wing and a tower to the Jacobean structure. When he died, his wife 'reverted to type' as Hine phrased it, and retired to a cottage. The hall and estate remained in the Alington family until the First Garden City Company acquired the land in 1873.

Some of Alington's fields are now under the roads of Letchworth Garden City, others were turned into a golf course. Letchworth Hall is a hotel, as it has been since early this century. My bank manager took me out to lunch there once. The Revd John Alington's spirit must be very bored. There were a lot of local businessmen enjoying their food, but no wild revelry.

Alington was a nonconformist. Nonconformists – with a big 'N' – and Dissenters of all kinds have had in the past a hard time around here. John Bunyan, the author of *Pilgrim's Progress* (1678), spent twelve years in Bedford Gaol in the reign of Charles II. He had been converted from a life of pleasure to a life of preaching the Word, somewhere in the fields that lead out of Bedfordshire towards Hitchin. The only surviving contemporary portrait of Bunyan, painted in 1684 and now in the National Portrait Gallery, came from an old house in Wheathampstead.

There are many places in the county that claim association with Bunyan; as an old man he preached to crowds of people in Wain Wood near Preston, coming out from the Baptist chapel in Tilehouse Street, Hitchin, where there is a chair said to have been given by him. The house on the edge of Wain Wood is called Bunyan's Cottage still. At Coleman Green, at a crossroads on a stretch of Roman road leading to the river Lea, there is the remains of a cottage – just the brick chimney, from base to stack, in an enclosure of plastic-coated wire netting – with a worn plaque on it claiming that Bunyan used to stay there. The cottage was one of a group demolished in 1877. The pub on the green is called The John Bunyan – but only since the 1960s. Before that it was called The Prince of Wales.[2]

The Quakers, or members of the Society of Friends, are first mentioned here in 1656. Quakers believed there was no warrant in the Gospels for a paid ministry; they thought tithes were unjustified, and sacraments unnecessary. They didn't hold with rank and hierarchy, they wouldn't take oaths, and they did not resist violence. This made them very unpopular with ordinary people.

They were most numerous in the east of the county. At Sawbridgeworth they were pushed off their horses on their way to the meeting house; the louts of the town filled the Quakers' hats with mud, and broke up the meeting house itself. In Royston, society was dominated by the Royston Club, whose members were local country gentlemen. Half a century later, Daniel Defoe noted that a few 'high Tory members of the Royston Club settled all the affairs of the county'.

The Hooray Henrys of their time, they mocked and persecuted the Quakers with uninhibited boisterousness. In Hitchin too 'I am afraid it was once the fashion', wrote Herbert W. Tompkins in 1902, 'to bait the Quakers ... they were regarded as victims who might be insulted with impunity.' Authority was on the baiters' side; the law officers also broke up Quaker meetings, the chief feature of which is stillness and silence.

Passing through Baldock in 1661, Pepys had a good supper and noticed that the landlady was a very pretty woman, 'but I durst not take notice of her, her husband being there'. So he went for a walk, and looked at the 'very beautiful' church. 'I find that both here and everywhere else that I come the Quakers do still continue and grow rather than lessen.'

The following year a law was passed making their meetings illegal. There were fines for the first offence, then transportation or exile for further offences. Since most Hertfordshire Quakers were eminently respectable, there was a shamefaced reluctance to prosecute. Some Quakers were transported to Barbados and Jamaica – but the meetings went on. In 1713, one Samuel Peet was holding Quaker meetings in his barn at Graveley.

Hertford – 'poor dead Hertford' to the Methodist John Wesley – was one Quaker stronghold. Its meeting house in Railway Street is said to be the oldest in England still in use. But George Fox, the Quaker leader, who was himself treated very roughly by the toughs of Baldock in 1655, did not think much of the Hertford Friends, and was compelled to deal sharply with 'Durty Spirits' and tiresome women among them in 1678. Hitchin Friends felt superior, and called their Hertford brethren 'light as chaff and bitter as wormwood', a 'loose pack'.[3] Nonconformists can be just as conformist as anyone else when it comes to internal politics.

Towards the end of the nineteenth century, there were rather fewer Friends than before, in spite of the repeal of the penal laws in 1829. The Catholic Emancipation Act opened career structures and a place in society not only to Roman Catholics but also to Jews and Dissenters. Many Quakers became less Quakerly. This had something to do with their prosperity. Quakers have always had a gift for combining philanthropy and highmindedness with making money.

John Scott of Amwell is the perfect example of this. The copious family fortune came from a London drapery business and from malting. Scott lived at Amwell House, a stately red-brick mansion built around 1730, the year of his birth. You get a very good view of it coming south out of Ware over the Lea; it is now Ware College of Further Education. Scott endowed the grammar school for girls at Ware, and paid for the new high road between Ware and Hertford – at the end of which his house stands – raised above the flood levels of the New River and the Lea.

He laid out extensive gardens, now buried beneath streets of modern houses. All that has been preserved is Scott's Grotto, looking rather woebegone behind its barricades on the side of the suburban road. Under the not very promising surface structure – a crumbling Gothic gazebo – and the overgrown surrounds, there are catacombs of passages and chambers lined with flint, quartz, shells arranged in patterns and bits of glass. It is open to the public at certain times: 'Bring a Torch!' says the notice. Dr Johnson admired the grotto, and was a friend of Scott, who was also the author of a long poem 'Amwell', celebrating the beauty of his district. His Quaker brethren were disapproving of his poetic activities; strict Quakers did not indulge in the arts.

But when at last, after the Emancipation Act, Quakers were permitted to go to the universities of Oxford and Cambridge, and could hold commissions in the armed forces, and become KCs, and Members of Parliament, they could aspire to be pillars not only of the community, which they already were, but of the establishment. My great-grandfather Frederic, for example, sent his son Hugh to Rugby, a public school; and he himself longed to become an MP.

Reginald Hine in his autobiography confessed that he sometimes felt repelled by Hitchin Quakerism – 'their guarded speech, their icy understatement ... the silent reproof of their better practice'. Also, he said, they had no sense of humour. Perhaps the Delmé-Radcliffes, who had not invited the Seebohms to dinner, felt the same.

Hitchin's Quakers are still active, though they would not claim to rule the roost these days as they used to. In the early 1950s W. Branch Johnson claimed that Hitchin still retained 'an atmosphere of calm and serenity attributable to their influence'. It is hard to discern today as you search in vain for somewhere to park.

Attitudes to religion, in the bloody and passionate Tudor and Stuart periods, can only be apprehended by us if we think about modern Ireland, and even then we are only half-way there. Hell and the Devil were real, and to have truck with the Devil was witchcraft.

Every period produces its own pathology. From the late 1500s until the early 1800s, unpopular or eccentric people – nearly always women – were blamed for everything frightening or incomprehensible that happened, and called witches. Since most people, including the alleged witches, believed in the power of witchcraft, some of them fulfilled popular expectation and behaved like witches – or rather, as witches were supposed to behave.

This happened throughout the so-called civilized world; by British standards, Hertfordshire had its full quota of witches, and was early into the horrible game. By a statute of 1563, during the reign of Elizabeth I, witchcraft became a felony, and the second offence was punishable by death.

In 1595 John and Joane Newell, a married couple from Barnet, were arraigned with Helen Calles of Braynford as 'three detestable witches'. Joan White was executed at Hertford in 1590 for causing deaths by witchcraft. In 1606 an 'honest fellow' was drinking with friends in Royston when Johanna Harrison came in and 'stood gloating upon them'. The honest fellow went home, and became ill; Johanna was charged with being a witch.

Witches were notoriously in touch with the Devil, who tended to materialize as an animal. A sceptic published in 1648 a waggish brochure called 'The Devil seen at St Albans, Being a true Relation how the Devill was seen there in a Cellar, in the likeness of a Ram; and how a Butcher came and cut his throat, and sold some of it, and dressed the rest for himselfe, inviting many to supper, who did eat of it'. This piece of irony, parodying sensational tracts and popular delusions, did no good. Two witches were put to death at St Albans the very next year, and the sensational publications continued; one printed in London in 1669, called 'Hartford-shire Wonder, or, Strange News from Ware' told the story of Jane Stretton who was 'visited in a strange kind of manner by extraordinary and unusual fits'.

In this atmosphere, any hysteria or mental disturbance might be categorized as witchcraft, and dubious 'experts' were called in to treat the problem. One such expert was a Hitchin apothecary, William Drage, who wrote up and published his case histories. He told the world about Elizabeth Day of Hitchin, who could run up walls and across the ceiling with her head hanging downwards. Another of his cases was Mary Hall, the daughter of a blacksmith at Little Gaddesden. In 1663 she became possessed by two spirits who came to her riding down the chimney on a stick. The spirits gave her fits and made her make animal noises. They also told her that they were sent by a neighbour, Goodwife Harwood – which was bad luck on Goodwife Harwood because she immediately came under suspicion. (To accuse someone of being a witch was a great way of getting them into trouble. Two years before, Frances Bailey of Broxbourne had gone to court to complain of abuse of this kind, and in 1669 John Allen of Stondon was legally indicted for wrongfully calling Joan Mills a witch.)

Mary Hall of Little Gaddesden was taken to see the apothecary William Drage, who spoke to the family – chiefly, one commentator believed, in order to find out whether they could afford him – but failed to help the girl. Then they called in Dr Woodhouse of Berkhamsted, another specialist in curing bewitched persons. He had also served a prison sentence, but no one bothered about that. To make his diagnosis he cut off the ends of Mary's fingernails and hung them over the chimney overnight.

One of the most famous of all English witch trials took place in Hertford in 1712. 'The whole subject of the Devil and his relation to witches came up again in its most definite form, and was fought out in the courtroom and at the bar of public opinion.'[4] Jane Wenham lived in Church Lane, Walkern, and was a washerwoman. A neighbouring farmer suspected her of witchcraft, and when a servant of his began to behave in a strange way he voiced his suspicions. Jane bravely applied to Sir Henry Chauncy of Ardeley Bury, a justice of the peace and the man we have already met as the greatest of Hertfordshire's historians, for a warrant against her accuser. Chauncy fined him one shilling, and a clergyman, Mr Gardiner, advised Jane to be more sensible.

But then Mr Gardiner's servant started to behave more oddly, and said that Jane Wenham had got into her head and was giving her instructions. Chauncy gave in and sent Jane to prison, with the zealous support of that horrible man, his son-in-law the Revd Francis Bragge, and of the Revd Mr Strutt of Ardeley.

Jane asked to be put to ordeal by water; this was refused, since trial by ordeal was by now illegal. But Strutt tested her on the Lord's Prayer. It was well known that witches were incapable of reciting it without stumbling. Jane stumbled. She was also in trouble because she had been caught stealing turnips. She apologized for this, explaining that she had no food and no money. Presumably the wives of Walkern's farmers and brewers were scared to give her their linen to wash.

She made some sort of muddled confession to the zealous clergymen, and came to trial at Hertford Assizes, though all she was accused of in the packed-out courtroom was dealing with a spirit in the form of a cat. Arthur Chauncy, Sir Henry's son, was one of those who gave evidence against her. The illustrious Chauncy family do not come well out of this story.

I do not know whether Sir Henry Chauncy believed in witches. But he devotes nearly eleven close-written pages of his history of Hertfordshire to describing in detail, and with gusto, the religious rituals accompanying ordeals by fire, by water and by battle, made lawful by an act of 1201 to determine guilt not only in the question of witchcraft. In the ordeal by fire, the party accused 'did bear an hot Iron in his Hand, nine Foot from the Stake to the Mark ... or else walked barefooted and blindfolded, between certain Ploughshares, red hot, placed at some Distance, according to the usual Manner'. This ordeal was only for 'Noblemen and Women, and such as were freeborn'. If after three days the burn had not healed, if 'any corruption or raw Flesh appeared where the Iron touched it', the man who had carried the red-hot iron bar was condemned as guilty. If the barefoot, blindfolded victim stumbled between the red-hot ploughshares 'without Hurt of his Feet', he was adjudged innocent. But if he got burned he was reckoned to be guilty 'according to the Proportion and Quantity of the Burning'.

The ordeal by water was for farmers and labourers, 'and was of two sorts, either by hot Water or cold Water'. There was also trial by 'Battel', or battle, which was a sort of duel with staves; and if the accused man could defend himself till dusk, or as Chauncy put it 'until the stars may be seen in the Firmament', then he was free.

But to return to Jane Wenham. She must have had a poor opinion of the due process of the courts if she would have preferred trial by ordeal. But she got a sensible judge. When she was accused in court of flying, Justice Powell drily pointed out that there was no law against it. Nevertheless the jury found her guilty of being a witch. Justice Powell condemned her, but saw to it that she was reprieved. Colonel Plumer of New Place, Gilston, took her under his protection; when he died, she was looked after by the Earl and Countess Cowper. I do not know whether she resumed her profession of washerwoman. She lived until 1730.

Jane Wenham's case was famous far beyond Hertfordshire. Pamphlets and broadsheets were published for and against her. A Hertfordshire doctor wrote a book about her, confuting the whole concept of witchcraft. Theorists came to interview Jane in her retirement. The Revd Francis Bragge also wrote a profitable book, justifying his actions, which went into five editions.

This was the second-last witch trial in England, and the death penalty for witchcraft was withdrawn in 1735. But as the authorities became less keen on prosecution, the ordinary people took the law into their own hands; this usually meant trial by ordeal, and as we have seen it was rough.

There was a shameful incidence of this in Hertfordshire at an astonishingly late date; it is said to have been the last known trial by ordeal in England. It happened in 1751 at Long Marston, not far from Tring, right up in the north-western corner of the county near the border with Buckinghamshire.

A farmer called John Butterfield, of Gubblecote in the same parish, refused to give some buttermilk to an old woman, Ruth Osborn. She cursed him for his meanness. Shortly afterwards his calves fell ill, and he himself had fits. (He had been subject to fits all his life, but no matter.) He decided it was all Ruth Osborn's doing, and organized a witch-hunt.

Mrs Osborn and her husband John tried to escape by hiding in the church, but the villagers hauled them out. The Osborns were very old and confused. The people tied their thumbs to their toes, wrapped them in sheets, threw them into a pond and dragged them up and down in the water. Chauncy, describing the ordeal by water, says on one page that if the suspect 'continued for a Season without struggling for Life, he was presently acquitted as guiltless of the Fact whereof he was accused; but if he began once to plunge and labour for Breath immediately upon his falling into Liquor, he was condemn'd as guilty of the Crime, and receiv'd his Punishment for it'. On another page he says that those who sank were deemed innocent, but those who swam were deemed guilty. At the end of the day, in either case, one was likely to be deemed dead.

Mrs Osborn was quickly dead. Mr Osborn died soon after they pulled him out. A local chimney sweep called Luke Colley entertained his mates by prodding Mrs Osborn's body with a stick and turning it over and over in the water. Then he passed his hat round.

This was too much. Colley was arrested, sentenced at Hertford Assizes, and hanged at Gubblecote Cross. This, in turn, was too much for the lads of Long Marston, who regarded him thenceforth as a martyr.

I drove into Long Marston past the fields of Gubblecote and parked near the green, by the Boot Inn (the third pub of that name I had seen that day). It's a pretty, healthily alive village, with new houses as well as old cottages. A stream runs alongside Chapel Lane, and children on their half-term were fishing for minnows and what they call 'bullyheads'. The stream runs into a moat, which breaks into ponds around a tower – all that is left of the fifteenth-century church in which the Osborns trembled at the approach of the witch-hunters.

The door of the tower is open, and the inside is full of rubbish and old travelling-trunks, labelled 'Folkestone'. It is a fine day, but seems dark round the tower because of the shade cast by tall yew trees. The ponds look sullen. Close by is an old cottage which was certainly there when the old couple were murdered.

Fifty years before this horrible incident, Sir Henry Chauncy in his county history had written of Long Marston that it had 'a fair Chappel, where the Dean and Chapter of Christchurch in Oxford, who have the Impropriation of the Tith of this Place, ought to find a Curate to officiate there for the Ease of the Inhabitants'. The church must have been in a bad state already when the old Osborns took sanctuary in it, to no avail. The presence of a clergyman might have done more than contribute to the Ease of the Inhabitants, it might have saved the Osborns.

Now we confront one of the major hazards of local history. I found the story of the Osborns of Long Marston in many books about Hertfordshire. It caught my imagination, and I imagined it all as if I had seen it in the cinema. Then I picked up *The Hertfordshire Village Book,* compiled by the county's Federation of Women's Institutes in 1986, and found the story told again, but under the heading of Wilstone – which is a small village between Long Marston and Tring. Gubblecote, where Ruth Osborn encountered the stingy farmer, lies between the two villages.

According to the Wilstone Women's Institute, it was the Wilstone inhabitants who persecuted Mrs Osborn, giving public notice at the major markets around that she and her husband would be publicly ducked at Wilstone on 21 April 1751. The old couple took refuge in the workhouse at Tring, where hostile crowds assembled, so that the workhouse-master hustled them into the vestry of the church. The crowd of about four thousand dragged them from the church to a muddy pond in Wilstone, now filled in.

Luke Colley the sadistic chimney sweep occurs in both accounts; in the Wilstone story, he was tried at Tring and 108 troopers of the Horse Guards hung him in chains in Luke's Lane, Gubblecote. 'Until the wartime airfield at Marsworth necessitated the widening of the lane, many tales were told of strange happenings at this spot' – Colley was supposed to rattle his chains at nocturnal travellers.

Chain-rattling apart, the Wilstone account is likely to be accurate on account of the amount of circumstantial detail it includes – dates, numbers, even the names of the workhouse-master and the police constable at Tring. Research into the Tring court records would resolve the problem. I shall leave it unresolved, as a warning to myself and others not to trust anecdotal history, or indeed any narrative history however confidently written – and least of all one's own intuitions and 'feelings' about a place where something awful may – or may not – have happened. One may however take comfort from the view of Claude Lévi-Strauss, social anthropologist and father of structuralism, that a myth is the sum total of all its variants. Myth is part of religion, superstition, history, hearsay and folklore. History, says the travel-writer Norman Lewis, turns out to be 'a fable agreed upon'.

8

TOUR

❧ ❧

The M1 is the most thunderous motorway, carrying the longest, heaviest and noisiest trucks, and the M25 never rests, except when a ten-mile tailback immobilizes its traffic. But the A1(M) is Hertfordshire's significant motorway because it is her spine. The route it roughly follows has been a north–south highway through the middle of the county for a long time, which is perhaps why it seems to mark a psychological divide. This is particularly true in the south and middle of the county; Watford, Rickmansworth, St Albans, Hemel Hempstead, Berkhamsted and Tring, in the west, have a quite different 'colour' in the mind, for a Hertfordshire person, than Hertford, Ware and Bishop's Stortford in the east. The psychological divide is less felt in the larger north-eastern section of the county. Hitchin, just west of the A1(M), has the same emotional 'colour' as Walkern or Buntingford to the east of it.

A glance at the map explains why. There is, in a manner of speaking, no north-west Hertfordshire at all; the slightly alien (to me) western bit is prematurely lopped off on its north-facing boundary by a deeply south-swooping chunk of Bedfordshire, making it a fat peninsula.

But so far as history, architecture and natural beauty are concerned, this fat western peninsula is paradoxically central. Take the A41, old Akeman Street, and pick it up at Hunton Bridge, beside the Grand

Union Canal. If you turn left past Georgian Langleybury, now a school, weaving west through the wooded, hilly lanes, you come to Sarratt. In Sir Henry Chauncy's day the twelfth-century church, with flamboyant monuments in the graveyard and faded wall-paintings inside, was in the middle of the village. Now it is well outside it, at Church End, in the centre of a maze of field-paths, some of which lead over the border into Buckinghamshire; you are very near the edge here. The church isn't quite alone, there is a manor house, the Cock Inn, and a row of almshouses, 'built new' as a tablet says, in early-nineteenth-century Gothic style, by a Mr Ralph Day.

Back at Hunton Bridge on the main road, Abbot's Langley is off to the right. This is paper-mill country now; to the right of the A41, where the river Gade and the canal run together with the Bulbourne to Berkhamsted, what must once have been all picturesque is now a banal industrial area, mercifully interrupted by still lovely water-meadows. The industrial buildings come very close to the historic church of King's Langley, which straddles the main road, its High Street full of traffic fumes.

But up the hill to the left, next to the ancient friary (where there's now a school), is the site of a palace built by Edward I. Here in 1341 was born the fourth son of Edward III, Edmund of Langley, the first Duke of York, whose emblem of a white rose was adopted by the Yorkist faction in the Wars of the Roses. His bashed and gloomy tomb, covered with heraldic shields, and that of his Spanish wife are in King's Langley Church. Enoch Powell has argued that the tomb was not originally ordered for Edmund but by Richard II for himself[1] – a small point.

It's hard to realize now how significant King's Langley once was. It was in the rose garden of this lost palace that Shakespeare set the scene in *Richard II* where the queen learns the news of the usurper Bolingbroke's success. Richard's uncle Edmund of Langley is in that play too, as an old man. (John Ball, a rebel priest who stirred up the people against Richard II, was hanged, drawn and quartered in the market-place at St Albans.) Queen Elizabeth stayed here; it remained a royal house until the reign of Charles II, and until 1919 it was still surrounded by a 700-acre park.

The modern industrialization has diminished well before you reach

Berkhamsted, but the traffic doesn't get any better. The elegance of Berkhamsted's High Street is made null by nose-to-bumper lorries. But it has always been an important place, because of its strategic position on a Roman road at the southern end of the principal valley of the central Chilterns. During the barbarian invasions after the Romans left, Romanized Celts held out here for nearly a hundred years. There is a 'devil's dyke' up on the common, called Grim's Ditch – early earthworks, sections of which can be traced through Wigginton and into Bucks.

Berkhamsted was a key fortress – for the Mercians against the West Saxons, for the native population against the Danes. William the Conqueror made his way here in December 1066; he wanted to go to St Albans, but the abbot halted the invader's approach by blocking the road with trees. It was to Berkhamsted that the English leaders, and the abbot, came to treat with him – in the event, to surrender.

It is rather embarrassing to learn how easily William got his way. The Normans just walked all over us, for the most part, as had the Romans. Chauncy in 1700 wrote that the English nobles agreed to meet William, while plotting to 'free themselves from the Slavery of the Norman Yoke'. William, 'fearing if he should not comply with them, he should lose with Shame the Kingdom which he had got by the Effusion of so much Blood', promised to respect all the ancient laws of the kingdom in return for their co-operation. So the nobles swore fealty to him as their king – and he immediately let them down and gave their lands and estates to pushy Normans, keeping a good many for himself.

He gave Berkhamsted to his half-brother Robert de Mortain, who fortified it with a double ditch and ramparts. Lords of the manor in Hertfordshire recorded at the time of the Domesday Book and for the next four generations are brazenly French. Among the most powerful and pluralistic were Goisbert de Beauvais, Jeoffrey de Magnaville, Peter de Valognes, Ralph de Limesie, Count Eustace of Boulogne, Bishop Odo of Bayeux.

I've no doubt modern scholarship gives the story of the Conquest an interpretation for our times, but I like the gloss put on it by Lord Macaulay. In *The History of England* (1864) Macaulay fulminates about how English villeins became slaves to French tyrants:

The subjugation of a nation by a nation has seldom, even in Asia, been more complete. The country was portioned out among the captains of the invaders. Strong military institutions, closely connected with the institution of property, enabled the foreign conquerors to oppress the children of the soil. A cruel penal code, cruelly enforced, guarded the privileges, and even the sports, of the alien tyrants.

Some of us fought back, a bit. Outlaws took to the woods and waged guerrilla war on the usurpers. 'Assassination was an event of daily occurrence. Many Normans suddenly disappeared, without trace.' Hertfordshire's native leaders made life hard for the occupying forces, especially in the north-east, which is why the Normans built most of their castles in that area. The mottes and moats remain – at Benington, Walkern, Therfield, Wymondley, Pirton and Anstey, for example.

As with the Romans, the English intermarried with the invaders and after a few generations the blood was thoroughly mixed. But Macaulay made the point that for a century and a half after the Conquest, English history was not English at all. We were colonials. He thought it was pathetic and craven how we hailed as our own the French kings' military triumphs, 'as absurd as it would be in a Haytian negro of our [i.e. Macaulay's] time to dwell with national pride on the greatness of Lewis the Fourteenth'. If the dependency on France had been maintained, Macaulay wrote, 'the noble language of Milton and Burke would have remained a rustic dialect, without a literature ... contemptuously abandoned to the use of boors'. Only with the separation of France from England under King John, and with Magna Carta, does the history of the English nation really begin, according to Macaulay.

But it seems to me that the unique peculiarities of the English class system are a lasting result of Norman rule. An ironic deference to the property-owning caste got into our genes. Without realizing why, we still feel that English surnames with the French '*de*' in them are somehow grand, and if we want to convey that a family is of ancient aristocratic lineage we say that they 'came over with the Normans'. To claim that they were descended from native Dark Age Britons would make them seem not more noble but less – what Macaulay would call 'boors'.

Our class demarcations until recently have been based on codes that had little to do with merit and much to do with the inheritance of land, with manner or manners, and, more significantly, with accent and the use of language. The gentry have eaten differently, dressed differently, above all spoken differently. That's how they tacitly identified one another, and that's how the rest of the population identified them. This differentiation began, in an extreme way, with our Norman lords of the manor, who had French ways and spoke French. The judges who sentenced the native population did so in French. Any young Englishman who wanted to better himself had to learn to speak and behave as they did, rather as in the nineteenth century and later rich tradesmen's sons were sent to public schools to be transformed into 'gentlemen'.

I must justify this digression, which grew from a reading of Macaulay, that sonorous historian, by recording that at the age of fourteen he went to school in Hertfordshire. Aspenden is an extremely pretty and quiet village just over the river Rib south-west of Buntingford. The village street ends in a field-track; you cannot drive through Aspenden, only to it, and then back again the same way. Right at the end of the village, past the church, is Aspenden Hall, where an evangelical clergyman, the Revd Matthew Morris Preston, had his school in 1814. (The house has been rebuilt since then.) Young Tom Macaulay was so precocious that he had written a Universal History from the creation of the world to the year of his own birth before he was eight. But he was very bad at games.

In the twelfth century the wardenship of Berkhamsted Castle was given to Thomas à Becket, who became Chancellor, Archbishop of Canterbury, quarrelled with Henry II, was murdered and made a saint. The castle, originally of wood and mud, was rebuilt in stone under Becket's charge. A minor element in his quarrel with the king was his unwillingness to give up Berkhamsted when he resigned the office of Chancellor: the two were generally held to go together. Henry fancied Berkhamsted for his own use, and held court there after Becket's death.

In 1216 the castle was besieged by the King of France, unsuccessfully; he sailed for home. Edward III did the place up for the Black

Prince (elder brother of Edmund of Langley, and father of Richard II) when he became Duke of Cornwall (it is still part of the Duchy of Cornwall). Under Richard II, Geoffrey Chaucer of the *Canterbury Tales* was clerk of the works at Berkhamsted Castle, but it seems agreed that he was an absentee one. No one has lived there since 1496. The castle was in ruins already by the sixteenth century, its stones taken to build the great Tudor house Berkhamsted Place. The ruins were rented out at the beginning of our own century to Lord Brownlow, then living at Ashridge, who let it be used for local festivities and sports.

To get to what remains of Berkhamsted Castle, turn east out of the High Street and cross the canal. Pevsner in his volume on Hertfordshire judged that 'the situation is unimpressive'. It's certainly odd – the railway station was built bang opposite, just over the road. The castle, which has played host to such mighty people and events, is humbled. But it's worth seeing. There is still the double moat enclosing a dramatically wide area, and a high tree-tangled mound where the keep was. Low crags of stone walling, built of flint and rubble like Hertfordshire's churches, stand in the grass within the enclosure.

Up the hill beyond the castle are the great high beechwoods and windy spaces of Berkhamsted Common, six hundred feet above sea-level, the glory of Chiltern Hertfordshire, encompassing the great Ashridge estate. It belongs to the National Trust. There is a golf club up here too, and next to the grand clubhouse the Animal Welfare Centre. Hertfordshire is good on animals; there is the Cats Survival Trust – 'cats' including lynxes – in Welwyn Garden City, and the Wildlife Breeding Centre at Harpenden. The vast woods of Berkhamsted Common are alive with deer: one day I got out of the car and, only yards from the road, saw a group of them stepping elegantly away from me between the trees, one by one, like a *corps de ballet* disappearing into the wings.

On the same day, I walked round the castle, and young boys in blue tracksuits were running round the high bank between the moats, on their way back from somewhere to their school. It's no ordinary school. Berkhamsted School was founded in the early sixteenth century – originally a grammar school, and later what is known as a 'minor' public school – and though there have been constant additions, the original building 'remains at this Day very fair and strong', just as Chauncy wrote nearly three centuries ago.

The school's most famous pupil in modern times has been the author Graham Greene. His father Charles Greene was headmaster there from 1910. Graham Greene began his autobiography *A Sort of Life*[2] with the words: 'If I had known it, the whole future must have lain all the time along those Berkhamsted streets.' He recalled the great flinty Norman church, the canal, 'the watercress beds, the hillocks of the old castle surrounded by a dry moat full of cow-parsley ... the wastes of gorse and bracken on the great Common'.

In his adolescence he found a revolver in a drawer at home and used it, loaded, to play Russian roulette alone up on the common. 'Beyond the Common lay a wide grass ride known for some reason as Cold Harbour ... and beyond again stretched Ashridge Park, the smooth olive skin of beech trees and last year's quagmire of leaves, dark like old pennies.' After playing his dangerously addictive game with the gun he came back to the school 'down the new road past the ruined castle, past the private entrance to the gritty old railway station reserved for the use of Lord Brownlow'.

Another budding author, Peter Quennell, was a day-boy at Berkhamsted School when Greene was there, as was the future radical journalist Claud Cockburn, whose family lived in Tring – which was where the boys went when they wanted a bit of high-life, to drink at the King's Arms. Graham Greene recalled that at sixteen, 'I sat on a gravestone with Peter Quennell and we both read aloud to each other from *The Yellow Book* with a sense of daring and decadence.' Riding horses on the common with Quennell developed in Greene a 'love for the landscape around Berkhamsted which never left me'.

Quennell, in his memoirs,[3] recalled reading *Madame Bovary* with Greene, 'the kind of novel neither his father nor mine would have encouraged us to open'. Quennell's parents settled in the town in 1917, when he was twelve; he came to loathe the place, 'and used to employ the adjective "Berkhamstedian" to describe any scene or human character that I found particularly obnoxious. Today I see the background of my adolescence through much more sympathetic eyes.'

Quennell's father was a self-taught historian, overshadowed in Berkhamsted by other resident historians of greater renown: R. H. Tawney, author of *Religion and the Rise of Capitalism*; the Fabian socialists Barbara and J. L. Hammond, historians of the British working class; and George Macaulay Trevelyan, who was married to a daughter of Mrs Humphry Ward of Aldbury. Quennell used to bicycle up Stocks Road past Mrs Ward's garden and the fragrant lime-trees that bordered it in those days; there were also, in those days, innumerable glow-worms in the grass verges. As Quennell writes, 'today those delicate love-lamps have been almost all extinguished'. I've seen them by the thousand in Austin, Texas, but not in Hertfordshire.

But Aldbury is still lovely, owing much of its charm to its situation; its pond, surrounded by delapidated barns and weathered brick cottages with exposed timber frames and twisty chimneys, is set in a deep hollow, against a theatrical backdrop of dense woods rising steeply towards Ashridge. Aldbury is a strong contender for the title of prettiest village in Hertfordshire.

Back on the A41, driving north from Berkhamsted, there is a suburb called Northchurch. On a small worn stone just beside the church door is engraved 'PETER 1785'. This is the grave of Peter the Wild Boy, who walked on all fours and could not speak. He was found at about the age of twelve in a field near Hanover in 1726; King George I, visiting Hanover at the time, had him brought to England, where he was forced into clothes, and Pope's friend Dr Arbuthnot and other eminent persons were engaged to teach him to talk. But the Wild Boy would not learn, and was sent to be looked after at Broadway Farm near Berkhamsted. He wore a brass-bound leather collar, like a dog, with a plate saying: 'Peter the Wild Man from Hanover. Whoever shall bring him to Mr Fenn at Berkhamsted, Hertfordshire, shall be paid for their trouble.' Peter can't have been too unhappy with the Fenns, for he lived to be an old man.

Continuing towards Tring, if you turn left off the main road just past the hamlet of Cow Roast – where there is a particularly attractive lock on the canal – you come to the village of Wigginton, from where there are splendid views. Just south of the village is Champneys, the most famous health farm in Britain, established in its mansion and 170-acre park since 1925. A single room costs between £70 and £142 a night at the time of writing, which includes medical consultation, diet advice (but not à la carte dinner), water treatments and massage, exercise classes, and 'activities' ranging from flower-arranging to tennis coaching. There are, of course, countless optional extras.

Champneys was originally a Rothschild house, and the Rothschilds are for ever associated with Tring, four miles away. Tring Park – now bisected by the A41 as it bypasses the town – and its huge estates were acquired by Baron Lionel Nathan de Rothschild in 1872. Walter, the second Lord Rothschild, is responsible for the Zoological Museum on Akeman Street, which developed out of what was the largest private collection of specimens in the world. Tring in his day swarmed with exotic animals. Emu and wallaby roamed in the grounds of the house, and zebras drew a cart down the street. On his death just before the Second World War he bequeathed his collection to the Natural History section of the British Museum, who keep it open to the public daily.

The Rothschilds were good landlords, rebuilding much of the centre of Tring; and most of the cottages in Wigginton were built at the turn of the century for their estate workers. Tring's main nineteenth-century industry was textile weaving – silk and canvas, the extremes of softness and hardness. There was plenty of scope for the Rothschilds' philanthropy. The courtyards and alleys huddled under archways behind Tring's streets reminded Herbert W. Tompkins, poking around in 1902, of the slums of Shoreditch and Whitechapel in London's East End.[4] In 1931, H. M. Alderman found plenty of 'odd corners' in Tring; but to him too they were 'dismal'.[5]

Returning eastwards, it is pleasant to drive up across Berkhamsted Common to Little Gaddesden, with the Golden Valley and Ashridge Woods and Park pressing up to the right of the road. Little and Great (which is smaller) Gaddesden are 'lovely without qualification', as W. Branch Johnson has put it, and so are the many large, well-hidden old houses around here. I have never explored along the lane from Great Gaddesden to the hamlet called Covetous Corner, but it is well named.

Weaving continuously eastwards through the lanes one reaches Wheathampstead. If I had to live for the rest of my life in one of Hertfordshire's small towns this is the one I would choose. It is not really a town, more of an overgrown village with an outsize flint church. The High Street narrows down at a bridge over the river Lea. On one side the river forms a pool by the timber-framed Bull Inn; there are swans and, on one late spring day, we watched a sportive pair of yellow wagtails in the reeds. On the other side of the bridge is the old mill, and behind it a narrow, violent weir which deflects a shining sliver of water from the Lea down into a running stream. Just outside Wheathampstead to the south is the grass and gorse of the common called Nomansland; northwards across the Lea bridge is Gustardwood Common – and, on the right, the entrance to Lamer Park, once the home of Apsley Cherry-Garrard who went with Scott to the South Pole, survived, and wrote *The Worst Journey in the World*.

Going east (it is the direction I prefer), ducking under the A1(M) at Stanborough, and following the course of the Lea across country, Hertford, the county town, is reached. Hertford and Ware are only a couple of miles apart. Just as an Irishman cannot love both Dublin and Cork, so a Hertfordshire person has to choose between Hertford and Ware. I choose Hertford.

There has always been rivalry between the two. The bed of the Lea at Ware used to be much wider than it is now, wide enough for the Viking ships to sail through. They were stopped between Ware and Hertford, when King Alfred dammed the waterway and forced the invaders on to dry land. Hertford owed its existence as a town to King Edward, Alfred's son, who built Hertford Castle with stone in the early years of the tenth century, beside the place where the Beane and the Mimram join the Lea, and used it as a base for winning back territory controlled by the Danes. William the Conqueror further improved it, but the motte, the flint walls and the gatehouse that we see today are of later dates; and the ruins are now the framework of a public garden well set out with lawns and trees.

The Lea was the medieval highway, carrying people and produce between Hertford and London. But Hertford actually declined and decayed after the Conquest, reverting to village status, because the Normans used roads rather than rivers and Ware was on the Old North Road. It has never fully recovered, though the castle retained its importance: Elizabeth I, accustomed to taking refuge in Hertfordshire, moved her court here twice in times of pestilence.

'Hertford is not an important town, as compared with other shire capitals.'[6] That seems the general opinion. As a result, it remains its old self in spite of relief roads built in the 1960s which carve the place up in an upsetting way. But there are lots of houses, humble and grand, dating from the sixteenth to the eighteenth centuries, timber-framed, plastered, and classical brick, with overhanging upper storeys or elaborate plasterwork scrolls and garlands on their façades. Some of the old yards and alleys have been inoffensively made new, some are still untouched, their irregular windows set in arches and minuscule bays under wavy tiled roofs. St Andrew's Street is full of antique shops. I find everything about Hertford agreeable, including the art deco Addis factory. Ware's old streets and characteristic waterside dwellings are, I must admit, comparable.

Another pair of small towns, right over on the Essex border of the county, are Bishop's Stortford and Sawbridgeworth, both malting and milling towns on the river Stort. Sawbridgeworth changed a lot this century; some picturesque maltings, the subject of a sketch in Mr Tompkins's book of 1902, were in the process of being demolished when Mr Alderman called by in 1931. Sawbridgeworth and Bishop's Stortford are the shopping towns for the rich agricultural and, in parts, super-gentrified hinterland westwards in the valleys of the Ash and the Bourne (lots of fords) – Albury, the Hadhams Much and Little, and Perry Green, where the sculptor Henry Moore had his home, his garden and his studio. A forbidding notice in this inconsequential and modestly pretty hamlet now announces the Henry Moore Foundation. It is definitely not open to the public.

Bishop's Stortford was a great coaching town, being on the route from London to Norwich and also a stopping place on the more awkward east–west journey. William the Conqueror's castle at Bishop's Stortford once covered four acres – all gone now. The bishop in question was the Bishop of London, who had the right to use the castle – and the dungeon within it, which was where heretics and other unholy offenders were incarcerated.

Bishop's Stortford's most distinguished son is the Quaker Thomas Dimsdale, a pioneer of smallpox inoculation who was summoned to St Petersburg to 'do' Catherine the Great and her son. When he came home, rich and famous, he set up an Inoculating House, not in his home town but in Hertford. The father of Cecil Rhodes was vicar of

St Michael's at Bishop's Stortford from 1849 to 1876; the church is built on a steep hill rising from the river Stort. In South Road there is a Rhodes Memorial Museum in the house where he was born in 1853. Bishop's Stortford is nicely hilly, and though there has been some pretty bold and recent infilling in the old town there are still some untouched and almost rustic vistas – such as the shaky old weatherboarded building glimpsed up on Basbow Street from the stone stairway down to the Hertford Road. I fear its days may be numbered, and the next person to write a book about Hertfordshire will find it gone.

Two more towns that seem to make a pair are Hitchin and Baldock, on the north-western side of Hertfordshire's eastern bulge. Hitchin has been central to my story since its beginning, but Hitchin's known beginning goes way back before human habitation. There was once a great lake here; the remains of mammoth and woolly rhinoceros have been found. The Romans built and settled here, and there was a town before the Romans came. Hitchin became a royal possession before the Norman Conquest; William the Norman kept it for himself, and it remained a Royal Manor into modern times.

A town's stature in the Middle Ages depended largely on the establishment of great religious houses. Ware had Franciscans and Benedictines; Hitchin had not only the Carmelites at the priory, but a brotherhood in Bancroft and a nunnery near the church, on the site of the eerie little almshouses called the Biggin, with their curious wooden colonnade built around 1600. Hitchin's church is the largest in Hertfordshire apart from St Alban's Cathedral, expressing not only the religiousness of the town but its late–medieval commercial success.

The church lies low, beside the river Hiz, and seems to crouch. The best view is from Hollow Lane, coming down from high ground to Queen Street, where you see its embattled chancel across the river looking like a handsome frog about to turn into a prince. Until the 1930s no one could have enjoyed this view, since the space between the church and Queen Street now occupied by the open market was a medieval network of insanitary alleys and courts. The Biggin was on the edge of this; another vestige, now neatly quaint, is the narrow shop-lined path that encircles the church, called simply Churchyard.

Queen Street used to be called Dead Street, since in the great plague of 1665 not a single person living there survived.

Hitchin is surrounded by hills; in the short distance north-west to the Bedfordshire border the wooded Chiltern ridge becomes melodramatic (for Hertfordshire) around Hexton and Pirton. On the highest point of the Barton Hills near Hexton is Ravensburgh Castle, an Iron Age hillfort marked now only by ditches and banks, with cornfields flowing through it and the brilliant blue of bugloss and alcanet scattered over the headlands.

Baldock, so solid now with its wide Georgian main street, was not listed in Domesday; what there was of it was part of the village of Weston. It owes its existence to the Crusader monks, the Knights Templars, who bought the land at the end of the twelfth century (after they had aquired Temple Dinsley) and were granted the right to a market and fair – always the key to the development of a viable town. The Knights Templars were succeeded by the Knights Hospitallers, who built a lazar house or leprosy hospital. Leprosy was a scourge in England in Crusading times. There were lazar houses in St Albans (one of them just for leprous *nuns*), Berkhamsted and Hoddesdon as well; and the strange brick building, now a pub called the New Found Out, outside Hitchin on the way to Wymondley, was also a leprosy hospital. The lepers were contained, but not treated graciously. They were forbidden to drink from running water, and were fed on animals that had died from disease and on rotten fish.

If you take the road from Baldock to Buntingford, and turn off towards Wallington, you find yourself driving up high hedgeless lanes through seemingly limitless fields washing over great curving downs. There is something peculiar about the look of this landscape. It is East Anglian in feeling, but there is more to it than that. The parishes of Clothall, Wallington and Bygrave were never enclosed by Act of Parliament, and this area was farmed by the medieval open-field or strip system well into the twentieth century, in some spots until the 1920s. The hedgeless landscape would formerly have been dotted with the figures of men working their strips, like big allotments; now it is deserted during the months when the hundreds of acres of wheat and barley are growing unattended.

George Orwell, who sometimes attended Independent Labour Party summer schools at Letchworth, lived between 1936 and 1940, off and on, in the isolated village of Wallington. He wrote most of *The Road to Wigan Pier, Homage to Catalonia* and *Inside the Whale* there. There were buses to Baldock twice a week, but Orwell went everywhere by bicycle. The cottage he and his wife Eileen lived in, called Monk's Fitchet, is very small indeed, two up and two down, with dwarfishly low ceilings to the tiny rooms. There was no electricity or inside plumbing then, and nowhere where he could stand up straight without banging his head. The rent was 7s 6d a week.

Orwell and his wife grew vegetables and kept chickens, and rented the bit of green opposite the cottage – now nicely mown – to graze goats on. The cottage had once been the village shop, and Orwell decided to reopen it, seeking advice from his 'proletarian' friend Jack Common who had once kept a corner shop in Chelsea. Common, who was living ten miles or so away at Datchworth, near Knebworth, recalled walking out to watch for Orwell's arrival:

> I leaned against a three-armed signpost which read, To Knebworth, Woolmer Green; To Datchworth Green; To Bragbury End. From that last direction and very much downhill there presently appeared a solitary cyclist, a tall man on a bike. He could have got off and walked at the worst gradient. Not he. This Don Quixote weaved and wandered this side, that side, defeating windmills of gravity till he grew tall on the hillbrow and tall too that Rosinante of a bicycle, an ancient Triumph that could have belonged to his father.
>
> Fellow-countrymen, men of Herts, we made greetings.[7]

What the Normans called vills – or manors, or settlements – were much thicker on the ground in this now quiet north-east part of the county at the time of Domesday than in the southern parts, which are today overpopulated. Most of the vills survive as villages, with roads petering out in the fields. They have a withdrawn air, however well tended the cottages and gardens. The Chiltern ridge here is somehow austere. There is often less than a mile between villages – Therfield, Reed, Wallington, Kelshall, Sandon – and Rushden the most self-consciously pretty, where we once looked at a house, called inevitably

Rose Cottage, but chickened out because the roof, or lack of it, frightened us.

Ashwell, beyond Bygrave on the other side of the Icknield Way, is a village that used to be a town; it has a grand and glorious church, a seventeenth-century Merchant Taylors' school, a little museum in a fifteenth-century house, pubs that do yuppie Sunday lunches, and a High Street that is almost as perfect as much-vaunted Much Hadham's. The hills around here used to be studded with windmills, or clusters of windmills, but they are mostly all gone; the one at Cromer has been restored, and looks good.

Walkern, down in the valley, is a bigger village, with a sublimated pink-washed Old Rectory, a mill and a brewery, and an enormous octagonal brick dovecote with oval windows by the pond in the yard of Manor Farm. There is a ford over the Beane overhung by black barns, close to a church that was here before the Conquest. Going east, you come to Sir Henry Chauncy's Ardley, and to Buntingford and Westmill, another contender for 'prettiest village'.

I become incoherent in this north-eastern part of Hertfordshire. There are so many villages in the tangled lacework of lanes and streams, each with a story and each with buildings and a church worth spending time on. But there is a road to follow which imposes a discipline. It's a very useful one to know about, an alternative to the busy A10.

It is a mild old road called the B1368 running south from Cambridge to Puckeridge. It enters the county, crossing a field-track that is the Icknield Way, just north of Barley, which has an early Tudor 'Town House', or village hall, and where the graphic pub-sign of the Fox and Hounds stretches in silhouette across the road. Barkway is the next village down, and then the crossroads called Cave Gate, where the Devil lived in a cave in the chalk. From here on the road runs parallel with the little river Quin, crossed and recrossed by wooden footbridges, to Hay Street and Braughing – where the Quin is forded not once but twice.

Braughing, pronounced Braffing, was the first Hertfordshire village we ever fell in love with. People have lived here since before the Romans, and it feels that way. The main way through Braughing is called, with bald obviousness, The Street (as also in Wallington,

Chipperfield and Furneaux Pelham), and there is also something almost imperceptible called The Square. Braughing has two greens, a fifteenth-century church flanked by old houses with gardens sloping down to the Quin and its water-meadows, and a good number of what Herbert W. Tompkins in 1902 called 'tiny amorphous homes whose walls are perilously awry'.

It was to one of these that we lost our hearts. It said, 'For Sale'. On enquiring, we learned that the vendor was a Mr King, who lived in one of the fine old houses down Church End. We knocked on the door.

'Just in time, darling,' said Mr King. 'You can fasten my necklace for me. I can't seem to manage it.' So I fastened his necklace. Mr King, now retired, had been 'in the theatre', as he told us while his companion, rather glumly, made us tea. Mr King was very anxious to sell us the little house on The Street. He even offered to lend us the money to buy it with.

The surveyor's report was terrible. 'Amorphous' and 'awry' were understatements. It had been built like a cowshed, apparently, and was now not even fit for cows. So we didn't buy it. But someone else did, and it still stands and looks very nice so maybe we made a mistake. My Hertfordshire is punctuated with houses we thought of buying, or would have bought had they ever been for sale, or if we could have afforded them. They represent alternative lives which we might have lived and never will.

The alternative life that he might have lived in a Hertfordshire manor house ruined the life of Anthony Trollope's father. A not very successful London barrister, Thomas Trollope lived for the day when he would inherit Julians, near Rushden, from his uncle Adolphus Meetkerke. He even gave the name Julians to the house he built at Harrow, in anticipation.

Thomas Trollope's father had been rector of Cottered, and later also of Rushden, two miles away by field-track over Stocking Hill. He had married Adolphus Meetkerke's sister; Adolphus was a bachelor, and it was understood that Thomas Trollope would inherit the house, and the lordship of Rushden and Cumberlow Green that went with it. This meant a solid income from farmers' and cottagers' rents as well as a splendid home.

Then, in his old age, Adolphus married and produced a family. Thomas Trollope was no longer the heir. There was nothing to look forward to any more. Thomas became a depressed and difficult man, did worse and worse in his profession, and left it to his wife to support the family by writing books.

We went to look at Julians, trespassing as usual, up its long straight avenue. It's an imposing, comfortable-looking house, largely rebuilt in the 1930s, though some of the masonry is Jacobean and there is a lot of eighteenth-century work remaining. Evelyn Waugh called it Queen Anne. He went over to Julians from Ickleford Manor in 1945 when he was staying there with Randolph Churchill – to have lunch with 'Audrey James, variously called Coates, Marshal Field, Pleydell-Bouverie, a strained, nervous cross-patch of a woman'. But he said the house was beautiful, the wine good, and the garden the first that he had seen in good order since the beginning of the war.[8] Houses and gardens, unlike us, have countless lives, being reborn with each new owner and only sometimes losing their souls.

9

HOUSES

❧❧

Before the Reformation, palaces were as likely to belong to princes of the Church as to princes of the realm. The house called The Palace at Much Hadham, just north of the church, was for centuries the country residence of the Bishops of London. There has been a great house called the Manor of the More, or the Moor, or Moor Park, near Rickmansworth ever since the fifteenth century, when Henry VI's archbishop George Neville built himself an 'oriental' palace here. Henry VIII used it as a royal residence, and gave it to Cardinal Wolsey, who rebuilt it. Greedy Cardinal Wolsey had two other houses in Hertfordshire: Delamere House in Great Wymondley, and Cheshunt Great House, which was burnt down in 1965; old people's flats now surround its cellars, which have been turned into sunken gardens.

After Wolsey's death, the More and all its contents reverted to the king; poor Queen Catherine stayed here on her way to exile and death. Henry's fifth wife, Catherine Howard, also spent time at the More. Later the house passed to the Earls of Bedford and the Duke of

Henry was staying at the More for a month with his first wife Catherine of Aragon when his affair with Anne Boleyn was under way; she was here too, and left some of the king's love-letters in the house when she left. Wolsey officiously forwarded them to the pope in Rome.

Brocket Hall, Lemsford

Furneux Pelham Hall

Gorhambury: remains of the Old House, and the Palladian mansion

The Rye House gatehouse, beside the river Lea

Temple Bar, from London's Fleet Street, in the grounds of Theobald's Park

Black barns at Wallington

Victorian pumping station at Chadwell Springs

Cornfield at Caldecote

Monmouth, the natural son of Charles II. The Bedfords pulled down the old Manor of the More and built another house on a different site.

In 1720 it was acquired by Benjamin Hoskyns Styles, who made a fortune in the South Sea Bubble speculation; he remodelled Moor Park at a cost of £130,000, making it the grandest eighteenth-century mansion in Hertfordshire. The second Countess of Bedford had laid out wonderful gardens at Moor Park; Sir William Temple, diplomatist and great gardener, was so impressed by them that he called his own property in Surrey, where Swift was part of the household, by the same name.

It's a bit sad that when people interested in houses and gardens hear the name Moor Park, they are much more likely to think of the Surrey one than the Hertfordshire one. A later owner of our Moor Park, Admiral Lord Anson, hired Capability Brown to landscape its grounds, erasing all remaining traces of these famous formal gardens. Capability Brown (who also worked in Hertfordshire at Ashridge, Brocket and Wrotham Park) is usually cited as a great genius when it comes to landscaping and the laying out of palatial grounds in the 'natural' manner; but he can also be seen as the destroyer of marvellous older gardens which we would value very highly today. In the 1930s, streets and houses were built over much of Moor Park's grounds, though a 'tea pavilion' by Robert Adam survives as 17 Moor Lane. And enough remains to make a spectacular golf course; Moor Park must be one of the most splendiferous clubhouses in the whole country.

The great houses of Hertfordshire saw a lot of royalty in the sixteenth and seventeenth centuries. They were expensive guests. Queen Elizabeth I's visit to Gorhambury for four days cost Nicholas Bacon about a third as much as building his whole house. She loved extravagant entertainment, perhaps making up for all the bad times she spent in the county in her youth.

When Elizabeth was a tiny child, she was dumped with her governess Lady Bryan at Hunsdon, east of Ware in the south-east corner of the county. All the three children of Henry VIII – Edward VI, Mary Tudor, and Elizabeth – were reared at Hunsdon House, beside the church outside the village. What remains is less than a quarter of the manor house King Henry owned and rebuilt, greatly altered over the centuries.

From rural Hunsdon, out of the way and in anything but royal state, Lady Bryan wrote a pathetic letter begging for more clothes for the little Elizabeth: 'For she hath neither gown nor kirtle nor petticoat, nor no manner of linen, nor foresmocks nor kerchiefs nor sleeves nor rails, nor body stitchets nor mufflers nor biggins ... God knoweth my lady hath great pain with her great teeth, and they come very slowly forth.'

Lady Bryan was not asking for anything but the humblest of garments. Sleeves were separate arm-coverings which could be worn for warmth or decency with any body-garment. Most additional items were unshaped, devised from strips of cloth folded or tied for different purposes. A rail was a piece of linen gathered round the neck; biggins were children's caps, made from material wound around the head; a foresmock was an apron. I can find no reference for body stitchets, but would guess they were linen strips wound around the child's middle, under or over the gown, for warmth. Since the princess had 'neither gown nor kirtle nor petticoat' as a basis for any of these, it's hard to imagine what she was running around in. Maybe Lady Bryan was exaggerating. In any case, Elizabeth bore the place no grudge, returning several times as queen to stay with Lord Hunsdon, who was the son of Mary Boleyn. She also stayed at King's Langley, Standon, Tewin and Knebworth. Hertfordshire was her playground and her home county.

Hatfield is always thought of as the home of the Cecil family. But old Hatfield Palace had belonged to the Bishops of Ely, until Henry VIII swapped it with them for other lands. It became yet another house for parking his children; the two younger ones were educated at Hatfield, and the boy Edward VI was taken in great state from Hatfield to his coronation in London on the death of Henry VIII. Elizabeth was virtually imprisoned at Hatfield as a young girl, in the reign of her half-sister Mary; it was under the famous Hatfield Oak that she heard of her accession to the throne.

Visitors to Hatfield House can see relics of her time there – a yellow silk stocking, her garden hat, and masses of her letters, including one written when she was fifteen protesting her innocence when she was accused of a love affair with Lord Seymour. She had, at that age, very neat and perfectly legible italic handwriting. There are two famous portraits of her in Hatfield House, as queen – one, by her Court painter Nicholas Hilliard, shows her with a little animal, an ermine, clinging to her sleeve. In the other, her dress is patterned with a design of ears and eyes, to suggest that she saw and heard everything that was going on. This is called the 'rainbow' portrait; she holds a rainbow in her hand, beneath the motto *Non Sine Sole Iris* – 'No Rainbow Without the Sun', the sun being herself.

Young Edward VI, her half-brother, in his short reign after their father died, had given to Elizabeth the great house at Ashridge, where as a young princess she lived for ten years. Ashridge had once been a monastery, harbouring a sample of the blood of Christ, guarded by Norman monks who wore, according to Chauncy, 'sky colour'd Garments'. One can visit the vaulted undercroft, later used as a wine-cellar, which is about all that remains of the monks' house. After the dissolution of the monasteries under Elizabeth's father, the blood was analysed and found to be clarified honey coloured with saffron. At Ashridge the Princess Elizabeth was arrested at the age of nineteen on the orders of her half-sister Queen Mary, taken from her bed and carried in a litter, stopping at Redbourn and North Mimms, into London and to the Tower. It was after her release from the Tower that she was confined at Hatfield.

Ashridge Park, like Berkhamsted Common of which it was originally a part, is high on a spur of the Chilterns, as I have mentioned. For generations it belonged to the Egertons, the Earls and Dukes of Bridgewater; the last of the line was the famous canal-building duke, to whom there is a tall monument at the end of one of the long avenues of the park. The huge gardens are wonderfully kept up today, with technicolour tidal waves of rhododendrons in early summer (no, I don't like rhododendrons either, but in the wide green setting of Ashridge they have an irrefutable opulence), and tremendous cedars, oaks and firs. There are 120 acres of garden and park. It's a place where you can wander for a whole day.

The massive house, a romantic Gothic palace with every kind of arcade and loggia and tower and spire and battlement and cupola and cloister and buttress, was built in the first two decades of the nineteenth century after the death of the canal-building duke. It looks much older than that because the stone of which it was built is flaking away like pastry. The restored parts look smooth and uncooked. The new spire to the chapel is in fact made of fibreglass.

Ashridge is now a management college. Serious men and women carrying files and clipboards walk through doorways made tall and wide with pediments and columns, under the colossally high painted ceilings, past caryatids supporting massive marble fireplaces, to eat in the various refectory-style dining-rooms. They must, in their devotion to the holiness of business, be more like the original monks of Ashridge, who were devoted to the business of holiness, than any of the noble lords who owned the place in between. They are also more comfortable than those noble lords. Until after the First World War, there were only two bathrooms in this whole vast place.

Another great Hertfordshire house was Theobald's nearer London and close to the Old North Road. Lord Burleigh, the first famous Cecil – Sir William – built Theobalds in the early 1560s. Queen Elizabeth visited him there eight times, once for six weeks. These visits cost him between £2,000 and £3,000 a time. She liked to go hunting, and Hertfordshire was rich in parks – enclosed wooded areas where harts, wild boar, hare, and occasionally wolves were to be had. The 'chase', in contrast, was over open ground, for fallow and roe deer, fox, and marten. The game laws dated from the days of William the Conqueror, who granted himself the right to hunt more or less any-where at any time, while his more powerful subjects – nobles and abbots – had a few set days a year allotted to them. There are three hunting parks already designated in the Domesday Book – at St Albans, Benington and Ware.

Elizabeth hunted from Hatfield as a young woman, attended by a retinue of ladies in white satin on ambling palfreys, 120 yeomen dressed in green, and fifty archers in scarlet and yellow with gilded bows. Her arrows were silver-headed, winged with peacock feathers. No wonder she loved hunting, it was like starring in a Hollywood spectacular.

Her successor James I loved Theobald's too. He swapped the old brick palace of Hatfield for it with Lord Burleigh's son Robert Cecil, the first Earl of Salisbury, who was his chief minister. The first Lord Salisbury pulled down three sides of the medieval palace of Hatfield in the first decade of the seventeenth century and built Hatfield House, the present palace, in what was then the most modern style, at a cost of about £38,000 – most of which went on the extravagant decorations, furnishings, gardens and grounds. The north side of this great house is stark and stern and rather off-putting, rearing up over a bare forecourt; but the south side is sumptuous, with an elaborate loggia probably by Inigo Jones. I still like best what remains of the soft brick Old Palace; its gatehouse opens on to Fore Street, lined with old and curious houses, Georgian and earlier, sloping steeply down towards the former Great North Road. In the courtyard of the old palace the present Marchioness of Salisbury has made a knot garden.

The original gardens for the Salisburys' great house were laid out and planted by John Tradescant the elder for the first Lord Salisbury. By the early nineteenth century little remained of this glory. John Claudius Loudon, a gardening popularizer who founded *The Gardener's Magazine* in 1826, visited Hatfield in October 1825 with his wife and collaborator Jane. The gardens, they thought, 'afford little to gratify the amateur'. Everything was well maintained, but there were 'no rare plants, either hardy or exotic', and 'little evidence of such a love of gardening in the proprietor, as would be sufficient to stimulate and encourage his gardener'.[1]

The gardens of Hatfield House today, in contrast, offer a great deal 'to gratify the amateur'. The flowers and shrubs that the Tradescants – father and son – collected for Hatfield House have been planted again. The time to visit Hatfield is in the summer, when in the third weekend in June there is a 'Festival of Gardening'; the west and east gardens have been restored to the Jacobean pattern, and in their combination of luxuriance and formality are a pleasure and an education. The old roses are particularly good.

But for people interested in growing roses, and who want to see virtually every variety on the hoof, so to speak, in order to have a clear idea of form, colour, spread and habit before they buy for their own gardens, the place to go is the 'Gardens of the Rose' – the Royal National Rose Society's twelve-acre display gardens at Chiswell Green near St Albans. Hertfordshire is a rose county – the Paul family of Waltham Cross, and Harkness (between Hitchin and Letchworth) have been commercial rose-growers of international reputation for generations.

One of the most famous Hertfordshire gardens was at Aldenham House, and was made by Vicary Gibbs, the first Lord Aldenham, Lord Grimthorpe's partner in the restoration of St Albans. He died in 1907, having built up a collection of rare trees and shrubs which was one of the most famous in England. The garden at Aldenham was broken up after he died, in what someone who was there called 'the greatest garden sale in the world'. There were famous gardens too at Tewin Water (now a special school), formerly the home of the diamond millionaires, the Beits, to whom there is that extravagant monument in Tewin churchyard.

Most extant gardens of great houses offer varied pleasures; the setting is often as important as the planting. At Benington Lordship, on a hilltop near Stevenage, there are not only rose gardens but accomplished double borders – and the remains of a Norman keep and moat and a Victorian folly. The early Georgian house itself, beside the church on the perfect village green, has elements of neo-Norman fantasy to match the keep.

Benington is where the old kings of Mercia lived, and planned the defence of the area when, in the ninth century, the Danes captured London. Later, the Norman lord of Benington was a local potentate. Gazing over his moat – now filled with water-lilies – across the lovely valley of the little river Beane, the Conquest must have seemed worthwhile. There are other old and desirable houses in and around Benington, but the one I covet most is quite modest, in the woods at the end of the track called Duck Lane.

Another grand garden which is sometimes open to the public is St Paul's Walden Bury, which belongs to the Bowes-Lyons. I call it a grand garden, but when we were there there was an endearing quantity of weeds and overgrowth. The grandeur lies in the high-hedged grassy *allées* fanning out from the house, cutting deep into the forty acres of woodland, the long vistas ending in statues or temples. This was an ambitious eighteenth-century design which has only recently been restored to glory.

* * *

Back to the seventeenth century. While the first Lord Salisbury, contented with his swap, was building his magnificent new Hatfield House, King James I at Theobalds was enclosing a park of 2,500 acres within ten miles of brick wall. He also made a zoo, with an elephant and five camels. The kind of good time that James liked can be deduced from a comment on an entertainment he gave there for the King of Denmark in 1606: 'The ladies abandon their sobriety and are seen to roll about in intoxication.'[2] Hunting was what James I was keenest on in all the world; the hunting at Theobalds was excellent. But he was equally fond of his other Hertfordshire house, further from London at Royston up on the border of Cambridgeshire, where he insisted on spending so much time, trying to deal with affairs of state at long distance, that his ministers found government very difficult. News of the Gunpowder Plot was brought to the king at Royston, and the death warrant of Sir Walter Raleigh was signed here.

James's sojourns at Royston to hunt over the heath – where the golf course is now, and a track called the 'King's Ride' – were expensive for the town and the people living around. He instructed local farmers not to plough their fields in ridges, nor plant high hedges, nor let their pigs root holes, nor do anything to hinder His Majesty's ready passage on horseback. This was because he was afraid of falling off. He had a special saddle made for him, with a high back and front, to keep him on.

James I died at Theobalds, and it was from Theobalds that Charles I (who like Queen Elizabeth stayed at Hunsdon as a child; and you can see his cradle at Hatfield) set out to raise his standard against the Parliamentarians in 1642, and five years later he was confined as a prisoner in the Royston house. A relative democratization of sport came in at the same time. After the demise of the Stuart monarchs there were no more imperious royal hunters in Hertfordshire.

But until the First World War at least ten of Hertfordshire's great houses retained their enclosed hunting parks; Lady Cowper, for example, had a thousand acres of park at Panshanger near Welwyn. Parts of Panshanger were sold in 1919 for the creation of Welwyn Garden City. Lady Desborough, daughter of the last Earl Cowper, lived there until she died in the 1950s; then the romantic Gothic house, built in 1806, was demolished.

You can see a bit of James I's modest palace at Royston, at 23 Kneesworth Street. It was never a very grand place, being a conglomeration of buildings acquired gradually. The town has taken most of it back. What remains is a two-storey brick house with big chimneys, some of its detail of a later date. Old houses further down the road were the buttery, the kitchen and the guardhouse. The brick house is very pretty, but when I was last there it was in a very bad condition, with rotten woodwork and peeling paint. If no one else is interested in King James's house, I'd like it ...

Of old Theobalds, almost nothing now remains except a window and some brickwork in a gardener's cottage. The present Theobalds Park, divided from the old site by both the A10 and the New River, is a vast house built in the eighteenth century and added to at intervals since by the Meux family to whom it belonged. Now a college, it is very conspicuous on your left as soon as you are across the M25 (coming from London), which here follows the county boundary. King James's wide domain is ringed by trunk roads and creeping suburbia, in the middle of which the old park of Theobalds survives, bisected by ancient 'rides', one of which is Ermine Street.

In the grounds of 'new' Theobalds Park is something extraordinary – Temple Bar, the monumental two-storeyed pillared arch designed by Christopher Wren in 1672. It used to stand in the heart of London, across Fleet Street, the gateway to the City. One sees it in old prints of London, looking up towards St Paul's – and looking at the prints, one understands why it had to be moved. There is one gateway for traffic, with a narrow archway on each side for pedestrians. In what was and is one of the busiest thoroughfares of the capital, Temple Bar created terrible bottlenecks of horse-drawn carriages and carts. It was dismantled, and its stones numbered. For ten years they lay on waste ground near Farringdon Street until in 1888 Sir Henry Meux put the whole thing together again on its present site. It cost him £15,000.

You reach it on foot, through woods and down an avenue which is no longer the main drive to the house. There old Temple Bar stands in the trees at a fork in the lanes, but to one side: it does not look as if carriages ever passed beneath it here, and it seems wretchedly neglected behind its high wire fence, on which hangs a notice saying 'Danger Keep Out. Falling Masonry'.

I've just been re-reading *Bleak House,* in which Dickens describes what I am looking at now on its original site, in the mid-nineteenth century, in winter – when 'the dense fog is densest, and the muddy streets are muddiest, near that leaden-headed old obstruction, appropriate ornament for the threshold of a leaden-headed old corporation: Temple Bar'. In the same book he gives a contrasting description of Temple Bar in summer, this time as a sort of immersion-heater: 'Temple Bar gets so hot, that it is, to the adjacent Strand and Fleet Street, what a heater is in an urn, and keeps them simmering all night.' It is a long way from home. I do not think many people come to visit it.

Knebworth is another house of palace status, just off the old Great North Road and less than twenty miles from London. Knebworth, in the late twentieth century, means vintage-car rallies, fayres, pageants, 'events' and rock concerts. But there was an important house here in the fifteenth century, built by Sir Robert Lytton, Keeper of the Wardrobe to Henry VII. There is a picture of the old house as it was in 1700, with a castellated central section, in Chauncy's history. Chauncy called it 'a large Pile of Brick, with a fair Quadrangle in the Middle of it, seated upon a dry Hill, in a fair large Park, stocked with the best Deer in the Country'. It's in that 'fair large Park' (260 acres) that the rock festivals and so on are held. The present ornate mansion, with its turrets, pinnacles, copper domes and gargoyles, was (like Ashridge) built in the early nineteenth century, by the mother of the novelist Bulwer Lytton, incorporating some of the Tudor building.

Edwin Lutyens, the successful and now fashionable Edwardian architect, married Lady Emily Lytton of Knebworth; their wedding was in the little family church in the park. Later he did a lot of work in the area; his early idiom for domestic architecture, using red brick and tiles in an expansive yet cottagey way, fits very well into a Hertfordshire setting. At Knebworth, Lutyens designed the formal garden west of the house, and Lytton memorials in the church where he was married. He designed the red–brick St Martin's Church on the old Great North Road in 'new', i.e. nineteenth-century, Knebworth; and he built Homewood, a couple of miles from the big house, for his mother-in-law. A little further afield, he remodelled Ashwell Bury, and before the First World War he did a lot in and around Preston: a terrace of cottages in the village itself, the farmhouse near the ruined chapel at Minsden, and Langley End. Most importantly, he worked on the 'big house' of Preston, Temple Dinsley. This early Georgian house was built on the site of the Preceptory of the Knights Templars. It was so much enlarged and altered by Lutyens that it looks like one of his own. Gertrude Jekyll did the garden.

In 1935, when Temple Dinsley became Princess Helena College, it was altered yet again. It is no longer really a thing of beauty, just very large. A great many of Hertfordshire's grander houses have since the Second World War passed out of private ownership and become training colleges, country clubs, hotels, boarding–schools, field-study centres, special hospitals, or – like Cardinal Wolsey's house at Great Wymondley – the prestigious country offices or conference centres of businesses and companies.

Salisbury Hall, which is very precious, has suffered more than most. It is a brick house surrounded by a moat, originally built by Henry VIII's treasurer and then 'modernized' in the seventeenth century, with tunnels for concealing royalists. Charles II kept Nell Gwynn here; she gave birth to a baby boy in this house, and held it out of the window over the moat, threatening to drop him in because he had been given no royal title. 'Nell, don't kill the Duke of St Albans!' said King Charles. So she got her way.

The title was apt. St Alban's Cathedral dominates the land around Salisbury Hall, which stands a few miles to the south-east, just off what was the road to Barnet. Sir William Beech Thomas, writing in 1950, called the house 'quaintly isolated'. The M25 has changed all that, curving round it in an hysterical semicircle, which comes monstrously close at one point. The short drive of Salisbury Hall joins the narrow old road – and on the other side of the road, on a high embankment, is the parallel course of the screaming, roaring motorway. You get the same surreal juxtaposition in South Mimms churchyard, just down the road – a rural churchyard of huge unclipped yews where, looking at a great tomb carved with skulls, your eye is distracted by the whizzing traffic on the motorway beyond.

To the drivers on the motorway, South Mimms is just a service station (on the opposite side of the road from the village), and no one could make a home of lovely Salisbury Hall now. Its old walled garden and some glasshouses are still there, wrecked; but the place has an unexpected new lease of life as the Mosquito Aircraft Museum. In the Second World War the house was taken over by De Havillands, and the prototype of the Mosquito was built here.

Brocket Hall is more imposing, and has been more fortunate. You get a great view of it, through high wrought-iron gates, from the road between Wheathampstead and Lemsford – a big square mansion built in the late eighteenth century. The river flows through the park, swollen into an artificial lake in front of the house, as was also done at Tewin Water, and Wormleybury, and Woodhall Park; the river at Brocket is the Lea, and to get a further glimpse of this graceful landscaping, the weir and the little bridge, you will have to trespass through the gates opposite Lemsford Church, or penetrate the rights of way that run through the park.

Queen Victoria's foreign minister Lord Palmerston lived at Brocket; and before him, Lord Melbourne, her first and most beloved prime minister. Melbourne had been married to Lady Caroline Lamb, a beautiful, highly-strung young rebel with literary aspirations. She was madly in love with Lord Byron, who grew tired of her. His death was brought home to her in a cruelly dramatic way. Driving out from Brocket in the summer of 1824, she saw a funeral cortège passing. On enquiring whose it was, she was told: Lord Byron. The cortège, on its way back to his family home in Nottinghamshire, halted later that day in Hitchin, where the citizens were permitted to touch the casket that held his heart. One woman insisted on kissing it. Only Rupert Brooke, among English poets, ever elicited anything like this kind of popular adulation; and he knew Hertfordshire when he was an undergraduate at Cambridge, walking

> The Roman road to Wendover
> By Tring and Lilley Hoo.

These lines are quoted in every book about Hertfordshire. But the Icknield Way, which he presumably followed, is pre-Roman; and owing to the vagaries of the county boundary virtually everything between Tring and Lilley Hoo is actually in Bedfordshire.

Just upstream from Brocket is an exquisite house called Water End, at a ford where the Lea runs across the road. It was the home of Sarah Jennings, who married the great Duke of Marlborough; her family came from Sandridge. Smaller houses such as Water End have survived where statelier homes have not.

One of the worst losses is Cassiobury Park, which was a palatial Elizabethan house just north of the station in Watford. The name refers back to the pre-Roman King Cassivellaunus, and the house was the seat of the Earls of Essex. The Loudons were at Cassiobury four days before their visit to Hatfield in 1825, and were ecstatic about its grandeur, comfort and beauty, 'such as cannot easily be communicated by words'. They noted the magnificent magnolias, rhododendrons and azaleas, the roses and ornamental flowers 'disposed in masses', the rockeries, 'Chinese' conservatory and pagodas, the aquarium, and a kitchen garden productive enough to feed the household ('which averaged at least a hundred persons') all the year round. 'The buildings and garden scenery seem peculiarly well suited to each other, both are venerable with age, extensive, rich in design, and generally in the highest order and keeping.'[3] Cassiobury Park was demolished in 1927. Its staircase is now in the Metropolitan Museum in New York.

Watford has become the largest town in Hertfordshire, its old centre swamped by nineteenth- and twentieth-century development – though the great church of St Mary, crammed with extravagant sixteenth- and seventeenth-century monuments, holds its own. Part of the landscaped grounds that belonged to Cassiobury Park, with its lake and an arm of the Grand Union Canal, are now a public park. The rest is under the streets. The Grove, an early-eighteenth-century house a little further north, approached by a drive that elegantly bridges the canal (or the river Gade, since they flow as one just here) has been spared, though the ring road borders its land.

Houses do still disappear. Reed is a scattered, straggling village with no nucleus, high, exposed and cold in the north-east corner of the county. There is a pub mysteriously called The Cabinet, and on one of the village's outskirts (it is all outskirts) a bleak Norman church with Anglo-Saxon bits in it. Beside Reed Church, according to Pevsner and the map, there should be Reed Hall, with Tudor chimneys and eighteenth-century additions. But it isn't there. Instead, there is a flattened waste and a notice announcing 'Freehold Residential Development'. I suppose there is something to be said for anything that rejuvenates villages.

Another characteristic of Reed demonstrates a feature of the Hertfordshire landscape in an extreme form. Nearly all Hertfordshire villages have ponds, or two, or three; they also have moats, or remains of moats. Every important house was moated – most still are, partially – and ordinary homesteads as well. Sometimes the buildings they protected have long gone, and curved wedges of water remain beside green mounds, or lie stagnant in woods. In the county as a whole, there are over 140 residual moats, not counting medieval monastic fish-ponds and deer–ponds. In Reed, there are ten or eleven. It must once have been a very different kind of place.

Hertfordshire is already saturated with grandly housed boarding-schools. It's hard to know what should be the fate of big houses that no one any longer wants to live in. The current trend seems to be to convert them into private flats. Watton House, beside the bridge over the Beane at Watton at Stone, had a big notice on its gates when we passed that way: 'A Caring Restoration. Seven Prestigious Apartments along with a sympathetic blend of newly built bungalows and houses, all in a delightful woodland setting.'

Aston Bury is a three-storeyed Jacobean mansion with a Tudor barn; in Aston Church there is a memorial to one John Kent who was steward in turn to Edward VI, Mary Tudor, and Elizabeth I. When we went to see Aston Bury it was awaiting the developers – another conversion into flats. We ate windfall apples by the moat and admired the view from the garden side. Local historians of an earlier period raved over Aston's air of remoteness, and the beauty of the countryside northwards from here towards Baldock and westwards over the Beane towards Benington.

That's still true, but with a difference. The lanes around Aston wind as they always have, with a defiant disregard of signposting. But half a mile to the west is the ring road of Stevenage New Town, and within minutes of leaving Aston Bury you can be driving through seemingly limitless urban 'neighbourhoods'. This doesn't alter the beauty or authenticity of Aston. It is pretending nothing, it is what it always was. It's the juxtaposition that is confusing.

Some people still have the courage and the cash to take on a major house and refurbish it. Queen Hoo is one of the most romantic houses in Hertfordshire, in the lanes east of Tewin Wood. It is small as grand houses go, and early Elizabethan, built of dark rose bricks that match the tiles of the roof. The antiquary Joseph Strutt began a romantic novel about its history, but never finished it. Sir Walter Scott heard about this book from his publisher, who was also Strutt's, and completed it himself. This fact is respectfully noted in many histories of Hertfordshire, but it was not exactly the high compliment it sounds to have been. Scott's contribution – unsigned – to Strutt's prolix four-volume *Queenhoo-Hall* (1808) consists of a few light-hearted concluding pages which make facetious reference to the indigestible long-windedness of the rest of the work.

The family now at Queen Hoo are undertaking a mammoth job of restoration. The new brickwork on the side facing the road looks a little raw, but it will mellow. The best way to see Queen Hoo in all its (to me) sinister charm is from the back, where it looks over its small formal gardens across a long sloping vista of fields and woods towards Bramfield.

Hertfordshire is exceptionally rich in Elizabethan and Jacobean houses. Some, such as Almshoe Bury, are even earlier. In the villages, in the towns, and in the countryside there are countless comfortable gentlemen's houses of the seventeenth (Tyttenhanger, Balls Park) and eighteenth centuries. To list them would make this book a gazetteer; all you have to do is drive, and walk, and look. Hertfordshire's old houses have curious names – the Golden Parsonage, Bride Hall, the Manor of Groves, Great Nast Hyde, Pishiobury. Every village with its adjoining greens and ends has a House, or Hall, or Manor, or all three, or – two specifically Hertfordshire words – a Lordship (which means a manor) or a Bury (pronounced 'berry').

A Bury can be a mansion, or a rich man's house which was once just a farmhouse, or a very ordinary working farm which was once, perhaps, a rich man's house. You can't tell till you get there. Sometimes 'bury' is attached to the name of the village to make a single word, sometimes it is written as two words. Bury means 'stronghold', and needless to say there is usually a bit of moat somewhere still in evidence.

There is also a vast survival of cottages, both thatched and tiled, dating from the thirteenth to the nineteenth centuries. William Cobbett in the early 1820s thought the labourers' cottages in Hertfordshire were good: 'They are made of what they call brick-rag; that is to say, a frame of wood, and a single brick thick, filling up the vacancies between the timber.' He admired their 'neatly kept and productive little gardens' but thought these timbered dwellings 'not *pretty* by any means'.

Some of the cottages have their brickwork plastered over now, and sometimes the timbers too, and are painted white. To the modern eye they are decidedly pretty, and few of them, enlarged and modernized, belong to labourers. Typically, they cluster round the neatly mown village green, overlooked by a flint church, its tower topped by one of the 'Hertfordshire spikes' which, in the mildly rolling fields, guide the traveller from one village to the next. In an outer circle of the village lie the council houses, their design much influenced (for the good) by Garden City architecture. The inhabitants of the council houses provide cleaning ladies for the owners of the sublimated cottages, the few big farms, and the family at the Bury down its long drive, hidden by trees, its moat an ornamental lake. On a quiet evening, you can hear the roar of the motorway. This isn't any particular village; it is the notional essence of Hertfordshire.

In Norman times, the principal strongholds were built in the northeast of the county. From the sixteenth and seventeenth centuries, rich men tended to build their seats further south. Robert Morden, in his *New Description and State of England* (1704) wrote:

> This County has an incredible number of Pallaces and fair Structures of the Gentry and Nobility. From Totteridge where the County begins, and East-Barnet to Ware, are so many beautiful Houses, that one may look upon it almost as a continual Street. The rich Soil and wholesome Air, and the excellence of the County, have drawn hither the Wealthiest Citizens of London.

That is the whole point. Hertfordshire, as the man who disparaged my county emphasized before I began, is near London. It has got nearer by the decade since the villages of Middlesex became merged into the capital's suburbs, and Middlesex ceased to exist as a recognizable entity, cushioning Hertfordshire from London. Nearness to

London has determined not only the pattern of house-building, but the county's commercial and political history.

'Yes,' I said to the man, 'Yes, Hertfordshire is near London.'

10

WEN

William Cobbett saw London as 'the great *Wen*', spreading like a dirty sore over the green fields of England. But paradoxically, Hertfordshire's proximity to London accounted for its pre-eminence as an agricultural county. There was a ready market for anything we could produce, and the traffic was not all one way. Although we were the capital's rubbish dump, until this century virtually all the rubbish was bio-degradable and useful as fertilizer. Cobbett, riding through Watford, noticed the fields 'manured by dung and other matter brought from the *Wen*'.

Waggonloads of 'London dung' – night soil and horse-droppings, plus soot, rags, ashes, horn-shavings, fur-clippings and other manu-facturing waste – were trundled along the Hertfordshire roads and tipped, uncomposted, straight on to the Hertfordshire fields, making them, according to an official report at the end of the eighteenth century, the best corn country in the kingdom. Even though some areas were never made subject to Enclosure Acts, enclosure in Hertfordshire began early – with riots in protest at Northaw and Cheshunt, which spread to other southern counties. By 1904 the mean holding was eighty-nine acres, which was well above average for England as a whole. Nearly every fertile acre that could be under the plough was exploited.

Hertfordshire farmers, in the eighteenth century, also smothered their fields with chalk, and the county is pitted with the 'dells' resulting from chalk-digging. Labourers carried the chalk to the fields in baskets or on sledges, applying anything from 60 to 150 loads to the acre. The exhausted chalk pits were left to grow over, and the dells today are picturesque, with great beech trees pushing vertically up from the bottoms to great heights. Now gravel is our only mineral resource. The pits are sometimes filled in with rubbish. Hertfordshire is still a tip for the great Wen.

We have produced some pioneer farmers, such as William Ellis (d. 1758), an influential agricultural writer who farmed at Little Gaddesden. Arthur Young, another eighteenth-century farming writer and the first Secretary of the Board of Agriculture, had Parsonage Farm at North Mimms. Like many experts, he was hopeless at putting theory into practice. His own farm was a total failure, and he was unhappily married to boot. Sir John Bennet Lawes, who made his fortune by developing the first artificial manure in 1842, established the famous experimental farm at Rothamsted on the Lea in Harpenden. In the years before the First World War, the Prout family of Blount's Farm at Sawbridgeworth were attracting attention in agricultural circles by making huge fields of fifty acres and getting rid of their horses, using steam ploughs instead.

It was not only rich rubbish for the fields that came from London. Rich people came too. Much Hadham, one of the county's show villages, where every house is a 'gem', beautifully maintained, is one of the many villages that have provided a country retreat for wealthy Londoners since Elizabethan times. Its main street, writes Pevsner, is 'a delight from beginning to end'. Prosperous communities like this evolved as the Crown sold off its estates to the *nouveaux riches*. Although some great estates remained in the same families for centuries, property in Hertfordshire always changed hands with extraordinary rapidity, picked up, improved (usually with a park, the mark of status) and sold on by courtiers, merchants, and tradesmen who had made good.

Cobbett, riding near Hemel Hempstead, noticed the children of labourers' families acting as bird-scarers when the black Hertfordshire cherries were ripening, 'locked out of doors' while their parents were in the fields. When he called into cottages for refreshment, he was not offered tea or coffee but an infusion of roasted rye ground into powder. Nevertheless, he had never seen country children 'better clad, or look cleaner and fatter than they do here'. It was London's markets that brought this relative prosperity.

Cobbett also noticed that the crops, even in the best parts of the county, were at least a week behind those in adjacent Buckinghamshire. I do not know if there is scientific backing to the theory that Hertfordshire is a cold county. In spite of its lack of majestic hills it lies high; and I only know that you close the car door in the great Wen and open it again in north Hertfordshire into a different air, far sweeter – and colder.

The urge to have a private park round one's house led to local difficulties. In the mid-fifteenth century, at Pendley near Tring, the whole village was demolished to make room for the lord's park. Daniel Defoe reports that a Mr Guy built himself 'a most delicious House', also near Tring, and then tried to enclose the whole of Wigginton Common to make his park. The villagers pulled down the palings and burned them. Mr Guy put up a new fence. The same thing happened again. Defoe didn't know how this story ended, but noted that Mr Gore, the present owner, 'has a Park, and a very good one but not large'.[1]

Many opulent monuments in our parish churches are to men of humble origins who left the grubby centre of London, where they had made their fortune in trade, and established themselves in leafy Hertfordshire – as they still do – to realize the English everyman's dream of becoming a country gentleman. This *nouveau riche* connotation is one reason why hospitable Hertfordshire, mercifully, has never been a socially smart county like Norfolk or Gloucestershire – though it achieved a fashionable splash in the early years of this century when three notable hostesses were in their prime: Lady (Ettie) Desborough at Panshanger, the then Lady Salisbury at Hatfield, and Lady Strathmore at St Paul's Walden (though no one really reckoned Lady Strathmore, say those who know about these things, until her daughter Elizabeth married the Duke of York, later George VI).

The businessmen and former businessmen did not want to be too far from the smoke; the fashionable area was the south-east of the county. The result was an early and grand kind of ribbon development on and around the Great North Road. There was horse-racing at Barnet until 1870 (and racecourses too at Royston, Brocket, and Harpenden; and outside St Albans the first ever steeplechase in England). Just off the Great North Road, Hadley Wood and Hadley Common – once part of the old royal hunting grounds, Enfield Chase – have survived as countrified enclaves of rich period houses within walking distance of modern Barnet (where all of a sudden you are in London, and a traffic jam). When in the 1930s Stevie Smith's young man Freddy rebelled against the muddy walks in rural Hertfordshire that she liked so much, and requested 'a change', they went to Hadley Wood. 'Hadley Wood, gentle Reader', wrote Stevie drily, 'is a built-up area with a wood in the middle. It is a change.'[2] Not all writers scorned Hadley. Radclyffe Hall, author of the banned lesbian novel *The Well of Loneliness* (1928), lived with her lover Una Troubridge at Chip Chase, a secluded, battlemented house at Hadley Wood.

Beside the Great North Road on triangular Hadley Green is a graceful eighteenth-century obelisk made of three tall tapering stones on a stepped base, commemorating the second of two Battles of Barnet in the Wars of the Roses: 'HERE was fought the Famous BATTLE Between EDWARD 4th and the EARL of WARWICK April 14th ANNO 1471 in which the EARL was Defeated and Slain.' Bulwer Lytton of Knebworth wrote about this Yorkist victory in his novel *The Last of the Barons,* as had Shakespeare in *Henry VI Part III.* Ancient and modern coexist around here without inhibitions.

Beech Hill, a road running west to the M25, with Hadley Wood station conveniently just north of it and a golf course to the south, is lined by an astonishing assortment of twentieth-century 'executive' architecture – ranches, palazzos, haciendas, châteaux, turreted baronial halls, Tudoresque and neo-Georgian mansions, any of which might acquire charm and dignity if given enough space, but which look maniacal all in a row. One major house in this area does survive, islanded in its landscaped park – Wrotham Park, built in 1754 for Admiral Byng. It is separated from Potters Bar to the north by the M25; and about Potters Bar itself there is very little that can be said. The huge wedge of the Canada Life building, its height and bulk more suitable for a city centre, has thrown everything around it out of scale.

Yet even in this unpromisingly suburbanized bit of Hertfordshire one must never be dismissive. Between Barnet and Potters Bar there is at least one beautiful old house, the Duke o' York pub. Eastwards to Northaw (over which Lt William Leefe Robinson in 1916 brought down the first Zeppelin to be destroyed in this country, and won the vc for it) and Cuffley there are still country lanes and rolling fields and woods.

Cobbett, on the Great North Road through Barnet and Potters Bar in 1822 on his way to Royston, remarked how 'the enormous *Wen* has swelled out to the distance of six or seven miles'. This put him in a vile mood for the whole day. It was late January, not the best time for appreciating the countryside. Around Ware he found all the trees 'very shabby', and his eye 'incessantly offended by the sight of *pollards*'. After Ware, 'a mere market town', he thought the land grew poorer: 'The chalk lies nearer and nearer the surface, till you come to the common fields within a few miles of Royston.' He wasn't impressed by Royston either: 'Not mean, but having nothing of beauty about it; and having on it, on three sides out of the four, those very ugly things, common fields, which have all the nakedness, without any of the smoothness, of Downs.' But today the swooping slopes around Royston, whether cultivated in huge fields or devoted to heathland and golf course, do have the soothing smoothness of Downs. Not every change is for the worse.

The south-east and south-central parts of Hertfordshire still attract wealthy city people. South of Hertford and west of the Hatfield House park, farmland and woods, there is an enclave of rural, unspoilt, jealously exclusive villages – Essendon, Little Berkhamsted, Bayford – linked by quiet lanes, all packed with 'desirable properties' (some of them now country clubs and 'health and beauty' centres) within half an hour's drive of London. At Little Berkhamsted there is a high folly tower erected by an eighteenth-century tycoon who lived at the house called The Gage; from the top of the tower he allegedly could watch for his ships coming in up the Thames. This same village has housed two pop stars, Donovan and Adam Ant. The Grange, on the village street in Bayford, was on the market in summer 1988 for £1 million.

But this part of Hertfordshire has not been cheap since before the Conquest. It is still thickly wooded with the residue of the royal forests that once covered the whole area. It is here that Stevie Smith used to take her long walks in the early 1930s with her problematic German boyfriend: 'And all up and down Hertfordshire from Hertford to Bayford through Monks Green woods over the estates of the Marquis of Salisbury ... we fought and raged and also we laughed a lot and kissed and sang. But blacker and blacker grew the storms and the whole of our sky was overcast.'[3]

Rich residential fashion, emanating from London, shifted rather later to the south-west, on the other side of today's A1(M). A drive around the unmitigated affluence of Shenley, Ridge, Aldenham and Radlett (through which old Watling Street runs) will prove the point. This is wooded, hilly, tamed countryside, punctuated by stud farms (on Ridgehill Road) and seriously large houses in parks. Ridge has a nice squat little church, spikeless; nearby a fine old weatherboarded barn was, last time I was there, in a dangerous state of disrepair, the old tiles slipping off its roof like a loose pack of cards. But it's a relief in this self-consciously spick and span part of the county to see something decaying gracefully.

Shenley is dominated by the campanile of the gargantuan mental hospital, a 'mini-garden city', as Pevsner put it, in its landscaped complexity; in the grounds is Porters Park, the home of the great architect Nicholas Hawksmoor (d. 1736). The most endearing thing in Shenley is the little village cage, or lock-up, shaped like a bell-jar with a knob on top. It is sandwiched between the village pond and the tarmac car-park of the Queen Adelaide pub. It could contain perhaps three miscreants, uncomfortably. Over one of its small grilled windows is carved 'Do Well and Fear Not', and over the other, 'Be Sober, Be Vigilant'.

When access from the capital becomes too easy, incomers destroy the very amenities that they seek. Aldenham, a pretty village just south of the M25, fights desperately for survival, with the M1, the A41 and Watford (Hertfordshire's own Wen) pressing brutally on her from the west. From the road between Elstree and Watford there is a stunning view of Aldenham's assets, Hilfield (originally called Sly's Castle, a castellated affair built in 1805 for the second Earl of Clarendon), Aldenham Country Park, and two great reservoirs, one of them a nature reserve. Aldenham village is much smaller than Radlett, her spreading neighbour to the east. This is commuterland of long standing. South-west Hertfordshire rapidly became home not only for the bosses, but for clerks and wage-earners from the Wen. Much 'dormitory' development in this area took place just after the Second World War; Chorleywood, separated from Rickmansworth only by the M25, was described as 'one of the most beautiful spots in Hertfordshire' as late as 1952.[4]

The numerous remaining grand houses round Aldenham are mainly institutions now. This is better for what is loosely called our 'heritage' than selling them up for yet more suburban housing estates. (Rural Aldenham is, incredibly, only fourteen miles from Marble Arch.) Aldenham School is a public school of sixteenth-century foundation, but nineteenth- and twentieth-century architecture, beyond the village at Letchmore Heath. Aldenham House, with the remains of Vicary Gibbs's famous garden, is Haberdashers' Aske's School. Aldenham Grange is the Holy Ghost College. Aldenham Manor, renamed Bhaktivedanta Manor, has become a headquarters of the Krishna Consciousness sect; somewhat to the dismay of the local people, thousands of visitors descend on the manor annually for religious festivals. Wall Hall, a 'castle' of 1802, is a campus of Hatfield Polytechnic, its farm buildings and pretty stable-block rubbing shoulders with new airport-style functional structures.

Sometimes it is the institutions themselves that become obsolete. The old Bluecoat School in Hertford, where Lamb and Coleridge were pupils, was founded in 1683 as the 'preparatory' school for Christ's Hospital in London, its front ornamented with charming lead figures of Bluecoat Boys in 1721. At the turn of this century, imposing new buildings were put along the avenue where cottage-dormitories once stood, and it became a girls' school. In 1988, the whole complex was converted into 'prestige offices'.

The connection between metropolitan commerce and the towns of Hertford and Ware has always been close. The reason why the road from London to Ware was always so notoriously bad and busy was the endless heavy traffic of carts carrying barley and malt. In the mid-eighteenth century there were no less than seventy malthouses in Ware, supplying London brewers as well as local ones. We are a beery county. Benskins was the chief brewery in Watford, and McMullens in Hertford – where McMullens Brewery on the river Beane, magnificently Victorian, is the first thing that strikes the eye as you come down into the town from Bengeo. Signs of the great brewers' power and philanthropy are everywhere here; McMullens donated, for example, the great gates to what remains of Hertford Castle. Hitchin too was a corn and a malting town; in the eighteenth century two or three hundred waggonloads of wheat and barley were brought to every market, and in earlier days Elizabeth I claimed she preferred 'Hitchin grapes', i.e. ale, to Spanish wine.

The numerous maltings in Hertford, Ware, and most other Hertfordshire towns give the roof-lines a characteristic eccentricity. Malting is the process by which the starch from barley is made sufficiently soluble to be converted into sugar during the subsequent brewing; and there were brewers too in every town, and in some villages. In the maltings, with their lopsided towers like squat oasthouses, the barley is dried, soaked in water, and spread out to germinate and then wither again before being 'cured' by heat and stored for some weeks. Many ancient maltings have been demolished, many are still in operation, some are derelict and some preserved and put to new uses.

In the centre of Hertford, for example, near the marvellous 'meeting of the waters' of the Lea, the Mimram and the Beane – crossed by wooden footbridges, with a weir and a stepped waterfall – maltings and brewery buildings have been converted into houses. Down Bull Plain in Hertford, if you look left at the little bridge, you see beyond the bright barges another fine maltings marked with the name C. Adams & Co.

From almost any vantage point in Hertford, one gets glimpses of a modern structure in the forecourt of the castle – the Castle Hall and Cinema. Its shape nags at the mind, until the realization dawns that its asymmetrical roof-hood is a 'reference' to the malting towers all around. These are silhouettes that Sir Henry Chauncy would have recognized. Back at the bridge down Bull Plain, on the right this time, is lovely Lombard House, which was his home in his capacity as Recorder of Hertford, and where he wrote most of his county history. The fine façade is since his time, added in the eighteenth century; but he would recognize the ancient, irregular back of the house, seemingly not so much on as in the river. His house is now the Hertford Club ('Temporary dining rights on application to the manager').

In the long periods when roads were punitively bad, waterways were as important to Hertfordshire as highways for transporting goods to and from the London markets. The waterways could also be a source of danger; the invading Danes came up the Lea to Ware. But the Lea, Hertfordshire's most important river, winding its way across the county before it bends determinedly south to the Thames, has also provided a psychological and geographical defence; the great Wen could not easily spread its infection across this barrier.

Hertfordshire has lots of rivers, none of them very big or grand, some of them not much more than streams, clear-running ditches, or what in America or Australia would be called creeks. The little ones sometimes disappear into 'swallow-holes' in the chalk. The clean streams and the pools where they rise are invariably fringed with watercress, which is still cultivated and marketed but is not the major rural industry it was once when thousands of baskets of Hertfordshire watercress used to be taken to the London markets. Our rivers include the Colne, the Ver, the Ivel, the Chess, the Gade, the Ash, the Hiz, the Quin, the Rhee, the Bulbourne, the Mimram, the Rime, the Beane, the Rib, the Stort. Some of their beginnings are worth tracing. The Hiz, flowing so urbanely through Hitchin between the church and the new market, is born from a spring-fed pool only a few miles away at Wellhead, a deeply atmospheric junction of lanes where there is a farm and a bulging black barn at the roadside.

One way from Wellhead runs past ancient Maydencroft Manor to Gosmore (where there is tall Avenue Farm, with an impressive façade of *circa* 1700; and a perfect double-fronted small Queen Anne house on the green, Victoria House, which we once nearly bought) and on to St Ippollitts, named for the third-century martyr St Hyppolitus, a horse-doctor. His church is set high on green slopes, and is best seen from the bottom of the hill to the west, against the sky. Another way runs parallel with the infant Hiz to Charlton, where the Hiz forms a pond by the Windmill pub, and the peacocks from Charlton House – birthplace in 1813 of Sir Henry Bessemer, who gave his name to the process he invented for manufacturing cheap steel – strut among the ducks.

The Oughton rises at Oughtonhead. You get there down a lane which becomes a path from the Bedford road out of Hitchin. The Icknield Way is close to the Oughton here, both of them running north-west past Westmill Farm, with its geese and white goats. The walk on the wooded banks of the sunken shallow river, bordered by cresses, mints and wild forget-me-nots, is lovely. You pass through Ickleford, where the Oughton joins the Hiz near Gerry's Hole, a deep pool 'where Gerry drowned'. That's all I know about poor Gerry. There is a notice, advertising this tragic fact, as a warning to local lads.

The Mimram's source is beside Lilley Bottom Road at Whitwell, and the little Rhee rises in an ash-tree-shaded pool in a hollow beside the High Street in Ashwell. Sir Henry Chauncy in 1700 described Ashwell and the river Rhee 'which issues from a Source of Springs that dreins thro' small Veins out of a Rock of Stone at the South end of the Town, shaped on every side with tall Ashes'. It hasn't changed at all. I go on about these new-born rivers because there is a magic and a mystery in the innocent way they bubble up from the chalk, so astonishingly clean and pure, overflowing their gravel beds in shallow pools. It is easy to understand how in pre-Christian times wells and springs were considered sacred; they are still sacred, and it is shameful to think how, on their way to bigger rivers and the sea, they are abused and polluted.

We have not only allayed the insatiable appetite of the great Wen for food and beer, we gave, or sold, our pure water. In the early seventeenth century the New River (which is really a canal) was initiated, exploiting the springs at Great Amwell, where the Lea is joined by several of its tributaries. The spot is marked near two pretty, well-manicured islands by a tablet inscribed with a peculiarly unmemorable celebratory verse by John Scott of Amwell; the New River also harnessed the springs at Chadwell, between Hertford and Ware, where the pumping stations can be seen in the water-meadows below the road John Scott paid for.

The organizing spirit for the New River was Sir Hugh Myddelton, employed by the Corporation of London. Canny James I, who had already got hold of Theobalds from the Cecils, paid half the cost on condition he got half the profits. The New River runs as parallel as it can to the vagrom Lea to Clerkenwell, the water being originally carried from there to other parts of London via hollowed elm-tree trunks.

The south-east of the county is very watery altogether; the Lea Valley, running southwards, is pierced not only by the Lea and by the New River, but by countless millstreams and pools, reservoirs, sewage farms, marshes, flood-relief channels, cuts and lakes. The Lea Valley at Waltham, Cheshunt and Broxbourne twenty and thirty years ago used to be covered in market gardens under glass – miles and miles of commercial greenhouses growing tomatoes and cucumbers, and acres more devoted to florists' roses and hothouse flowers. This is mostly gone, though from the train – the Cambridge line from Liverpool Street – one glimpses a residual wilderness of wrecked greenhouses, with rampant weeds proliferating under what shelter remains and bursting out through the shattered glass roofs. The Lea Valley now is, as we have seen, transformed into a 'recreational area', alongside industries of a non-vegetal kind.

The extreme west of the county is equally watery, and has a short length of another famous artificial waterway, the Grand Junction Canal, the brainchild of the Duke of Bridgewater who owned Ashridge. It was begun in the early 1790s, to join the Oxford Canal to the Thames, with four collaterals. It was built from London out, cutting round Rickmansworth, through Croxley Green and just west of Watford, and reaching Tring in 1799. It associates promiscuously with the Gade, the Chess, the Colne and the Bulbourne, creating yet another aqueous maze of lakes and channels, which on the map looks like threads and beads of spilt mercury. The Hertfordshire section of the canal is short but, with its numerous bridges and locks, very beautiful, especially where it runs under wooded slopes between Aldbury and Tring.

The reservoirs at Aldenham were made in conjunction with the canal, and at the canal's highest point it runs very close to the Tring reservoirs, forming a strange, waterfilled plateau of a landscape precious to birds and to birdwatchers. The towing paths everywhere make miles of lovely walks. I like the lock at Winkwell just outside Berkhamsted, only yards from the busy A41 but hidden in a dip, with the canal flowing alongside the little river Bulbourne and a pub called the Three Horseshoes (dated 1535); and over the bridge the steep, narrow and tree-covered Pouchen End Lane.

At the top of this lane I am only a mile from Hemel Hempstead, whose modern centre is a paradigm for south-east England in the late 1980s in its flamboyant commercial successfulness. Cobbett in the 1820s found Hemel Hempstead 'a very pretty town, with beautiful environs ... clean, substantially built, and a very pretty place altogether'. *Mutatis mutandis,* that is still true; the canal, which was approved of by Cobbett, runs with the Bulbourne through the wide water-meadows here between the A41 and the town, softening every aspect.

There used to be a thriving wood-turning industry in these parts and also in the Lea Valley, making dishes and bowls, shoe-heels and chair-frames from the alders that grow beside the waterways. Baskets were made from willow growing in marshy ground at Wormley and at Hitchin, where the osier-beds were in the town at the end of Bancroft (where there is now a public garden and a recreation ground). Until the mid-1950s there was a shop in Hitchin's Tilehouse Street selling nothing but locally made baskets, owned by a family who had been in the business for generations. Baskets were essential, durable containers. But now we use plastic containers, and go shopping with plastic carrier-bags. About thirty-five acres of land in and around Hitchin were devoted to the commercial growing of lavender just before the First World War. This fragrant industry too has collapsed.

Industries collapse, or are destroyed, in our own time too. Just before the First World War, Elstree was picked as a suitable place for film-making, being near London but out of range of the pea-soup fogs. The trend developed, and studios were built at both Elstree and adjacent Borehamwood – Hertfordshire's tinsel town where the BBC's soap opera *EastEnders* is filmed. Films were made at Welwyn Garden City too between the wars, but it is Elstree Studios (actually at Borehamwood), founded in 1926 and the last of Hertfordshire's nine studios, that survived the longest. Laurence Olivier, Ralph Richardson, Charles Laughton and James Mason were among those who made their film débuts here. *Star Wars,* which broke all previous box-office records in the late 1970s, was made here, as were Spielberg's *Indiana Jones* movies.

Elstree Studios have, time and again, been threatened with closure. In summer 1988 it seemed that the end was inevitable, with reports that the owners, the Cannon Group, were selling out to property developers. But in the autumn the studios were reprieved once again. The new owners were the entertainment company Brent Walker, who planned to lure films – mostly TV series and commercials – back to Elstree. But the studios are not what they were; they are just 'four-wall' facilities, offering production companies a set but not the full complement of technicians and services which were Elstree's contribution to the British film industry for more than sixty years.

It was the Grand Junction Canal which brought the industrial revolution from the Wen into western Hertfordshire, making possible the cheap transport of raw materials. But paper-making, which like watercress-growing depends on an abundance of running water (and, unlike watercress, pollutes it), was a Hertfordshire speciality before the building of the canal. The very first English maker of fine white paper on record is John Tate, who had a mill at Hertford; his paper was used for an edition of Chaucer in 1498. In the eighteenth century there were about twenty paper-mills in the county; this number became vastly reduced, but the actual volume of paper made increased.

The first mill in England to make paper mechanically was also in Hertfordshire; a man called Fourdrinier introduced a French process that produced a continuous web of paper on a wire-mesh moving belt, at Frogmore Mill near Boxmoor, on the Gade, in 1803. John Dickinson of Nash Mills made a better machine, with a revolving cylinder of wire mesh, which he patented in 1809. He also acquired Croxley Mills (this book is typed on Croxley Script, and I used to use a deep-blue 'linen' writing-paper made by Dickinson called Croxley Cambric). At Apsley Mills near Hemel Hempstead, Dickinson made the paper for the early postage stamps and covers, and the stiff paper for the cartridges used at the Battle of Waterloo.

Hertfordshire has always been strong in the allied trade of printing. There was from 1583 a law that no printing might be done anywhere in England other than London, Oxford, Cambridge and, later, York; it was not until this ruling lapsed in the late seventeenth century that printing was possible in Hertfordshire. Stephen Austin of Hertford, whose firm, founded in 1768, was the publisher of the long-running liberal newspaper the *Hertfordshire Mercury,* became distinguished as a specialist printer of oriental texts. They were the official printers for the East India Company's college, which became the public school Haileybury College. Printers, with shoe-factories, were the largest employers in St Albans until recent years; Watford and Letchworth too have depended heavily on printing, and the Lea Valley towns are still full of printing works, though the technology has been revolutionized.

All these trades and services were and are geared to the needs of the Wen. Hertfordshire had another industry which has altogether vanished, but which is fascinating for two reasons. It evolved not because of the nearness of London, but because of the nearness of Luton, in the opposite direction; and it was a cottage industry that made money for ordinary women, giving them, for the space of a century, an unprecedented economic independence.

Luton, which is just in Bedfordshire, makes Vauxhall cars and Bedford vans; it also makes hats, though not in such huge quantities as in the past. The industry I'm talking about is the making of straw plait to be coiled and stitched, or woven, for the hats that were made at Luton. St Albans and Markyate have been hat-making places too; and a surprising residue of the tradition flourishes today at Weston, a small village near Baldock. Here, in what used to be the forge, are made all the tall bearskins worn by Guardsmen. The main works are given over to the manufacture of uniform caps; all the bearskins are made entirely by hand by one man, Mr D. Green, who was taught how to do it in preparation for the queen's coronation. The actual bear fur comes from Canada, and Mr Green can make between eight and ten busbies a week.

This is a highly specialized craft, and Mr Green is the only master of it in the whole of Britain. There's a limited market for bearskins, and the Ministry of Defence is Mr Green's only employer. But I've no doubt that straw has been used to make hats ever since anyone wore hats at all, even though until the eighteenth century straw hats and bonnets were worn in England by country women and servant girls, not by 'ladies'. Pepys, staying at Hatfield in 1667, wrote in his diary how the ladies in his party 'had the pleasure of putting on some straw hats, which are much worn in this country [i.e. in this area], and did become them mightily, especially my wife'.

A few decades later, everyone was wearing straw hats. The women and children who plaited the straw earned as much as the men did in the fields. Arthur Young, in his *General View of Agriculture of Hertfordshire* (1804), wrote that plaiting was unpopular with farmers because increased earnings made the poor 'saucy', and the women 'averse to husbandry' and unwilling to go into domestic service. If industries like this had survived, women's liberation might have come sooner.

Older women taught the art in plaiting schools in the villages – it took about five weeks to learn. In the early nineteenth century Hitchin children were kept from ordinary school to do this work, and so knew absolutely nothing except how to plait.

Every district had its own peculiar plait, with a special name. Hitchin's was 'broad twist', among others. Berkhamsted's plait had fancy names – China Pearl, Rock Coburg, Moss Edge. The wheat for the straw had to be reaped by hand, as a machine would ruin the stems. Certain varieties of wheat were grown specifically for the quality of their straw, which was cut when the ear was still unripe and the stalks bright. Each stalk was divided with a knife longwise into anything between four and nine parts; this fiddly process was speeded up by the invention of a 'splitter'. The plaiter held the ends in her mouth as she worked, producing plait in twenty-yard lengths which she wound round her left wrist. The plait was then flattened in the rollers of a special little mangle. (You can see the tools of this trade preserved in Hitchin Museum.) Finally the plait was bleached in sulphur fumes, and sold in plait-markets in the streets and market-places.

It is the usual story: a local industry ruined by cheap imports. In September 1829, Cobbett was in Tring ('a very pretty and respectable place'), and at the door of a shop he noticed 'a large *case,* with the lid taken off, containing *bundles of straw for platting*. It was straw of spring wheat, tied up in small bundles, with the ear on.' Cobbett asked the shopkeeper where he got this straw, and was told that it came from Tuscany. 'I told the shopkeeper, that I wonder that they should send to Tuscany for the straw, seeing that it might be grown, harvested, and equally well bleached at Tring.' All the local people had to do, he said, was to read his book *Cottage Economy,* paragraphs 224 to 234 inclusive, 'where they will find, as plain as words can make it, the whole mass of directions for taking the seed of the wheat, and converting the produce into bonnets'.

There was worse to come. From the 1860s, hatters began importing not just Italian straw but Italian straw plait, and then Japanese straw plait, which was not only cheaper but lighter and whiter. Hatters in St Albans brought in palm leaves from Cuba, and taught the village women to weave them like a basket. But while the hat industry as a whole flourished under these expansive new circumstances, Hertfordshire's cottage industry was ultimately doomed.

Herbert W. Tompkins, wandering around Hemel Hempstead in 1902, wrote that 'These last few days I have sometimes seen a woman or child plaiting before their cottage, but 20 years ago I met them everywhere, holding the short straws between their teeth, and plaiting swiftly and deftly as they talked.' By 1908, village girls were working in the Luton hat-factories, making up hats from the foreign plait; and a writer in *The Connoisseur* in 1910 reported:

> Some 55 years ago, when staying at Wymondely, near Hitchin, I noted that nearly all the women and children at the cottage doors or walking along the roads were plaiting straw. Then the price was good, so much so that many men forsook farm work and devoted their time to plaiting; and this was the general custom for many miles around that district. Today the young cannot plait, and only a few veterans of the art are left.

By the end of the First World War, the art was virtually extinct.

The Wen increasingly affects every aspect of life in Hertfordshire. For a long time firms and institutions have had to pay 'London weighting' to their employees in the capital, because of the high cost of housing there. In the past few years they have had to acknowledge a wider high-cost area, known as Roseland: the 'Rose' part is an acronym for 'Rest Of the South-East'. Hertfordshire is in Roseland, and shares in the soaring property values that have characterized the 1980s. House prices in and around St Albans, for example – within spitting distance of three motorways, and eighteen minutes from the City by the fast train – are now ahead of those in stockbroker Surrey; and Welwyn Garden City, twenty-five minutes from King's Cross, has recently overtaken St Albans as the most expensive place anywhere outside London in which to buy a home. Old inhabitants are tempted to cash in and remove themselves to Bedfordshire or Lincolnshire. There is a huge pressure to release land for building. The Green Belt, which has saved us so far, and made Hertfordshire's real countryside quicker to reach than that of any county to the west, east or south of London's sprawling suburbs, may not survive this pressure.

Of course the *whole* county will never be built up. The worst that could happen is not conurbation so much as consuburbation. Hertfordshire would still be a more pleasant place to be than many, or most, on this cruel world's surface. There would always be trees and gardens, bluebells in the woods, big houses in parks, and magical enclaves of unspoilt villages with dovecotes, ponds and greens where the cottages, rectories and manor houses will be even more expensive than they are now.

Every development consortium and local authority makes plans for the provision of permanent green spaces. There will be leisure parks, woodland walks, country parks, bird sanctuaries, nature reserves, and plenty of water for fishing, sailing and swimming. You can see, already, how it might be: why does the pleasant bathing lake at Rickmansworth have to be called the Aquadrome? Why does the lovely high common, up Baas Hill and White Stubbs Lane from Broxbourne, have to be aggressively labelled 'Designated as an Open Space'? Presumably any space that is not thus 'designated' is in danger from developers; but these notices give the countryside a school-playground look. In a scathing sketch called 'Total Environment' in *Thompson,* her satirical programme shown in autumn 1988 on BBC1, the actress Emma Thompson presented a mock interview between Jackie and Max the planner, who demonstrated to her his model of the future:

> *Max:* Well this model is if you like the blueprint for what we hope will eventually be Hertfordshire, where there is at the moment a lot of old-style county lying about not being of much use to anybody, the economy in particular... This is what we call Landscaped Leisure Space – LLS.

Hertfordshire's a lovely place but at its best, it's *patchy* – it needs contouring which is what's happening here – you see flat fields contrasting with hilly sectors for walkers, three or four golf courses that double as picnic areas, wooded zones with evenly spaced trees for easier access . . .

Here's something I'm particularly fond of – we've reproduced an Anglo-Saxon burial mound here, which is lovely to climb in summer, but which at the flick of a switch converts to something rather special. See if you can guess what it is.

I won't trouble you with what it is that the burial mound converts to. Max terminates his presentation with the assertion that his Total Environment 'combines technology's efficiency with Nature's tips on beauty. It's the ultimate really, no smells, no mess, no problem, just gorgeous.'

Jackie: And do the people of Hertfordshire share your view?
Max: The what of Hertfordshire?

Does it matter? And if it does, is there anything the people of Hertfordshire can do about it?

This chapter is in the nature of an elegy – not because I despair of the future of Hertfordshire, because I don't. Something will survive of the unique human-scale loveliness I have tried to describe – the hard-edged quality of the light, the magic springs from which the rivers grow, the small surprises of the landscape, the secret hollows and the wide windy views. But by the time this book is published we will no longer own the cottage on the pond. The Wen has won – for the time being.

NOTES

1 ROOTS

1 *The Diaries of Evelyn Waugh*, ed. Michael Davie, Weidenfeld & Nicolson 1976.
2 *Victoria History of the Counties of England*, Vol. 2, 1908.
3 Herbert W. Tompkins, *Highways and Byways of Hertfordshire*, Macmillan 1902.
4 *A Suppressed Cry*, Routledge & Kegan Paul 1969.
5 Reginald Hine, *Confessions of an Uncommon Attorney*, Dent 1945.

2 ROADS

1 Lionel M. Munby, *The Hertfordshire Landscape*, Hodder & Stoughton 1977.
2 I am indebted to Thomas Burke, *Travel in England*, Batsford 1942, for some of the general information in this section.
3 W. Branch Johnson, *Industrial Archaeology of Hertfordshire*, David & Charles 1970.
4 Lionel M. Munby, *op. cit.*
5 *A Professional Hertfordshire Tramp*, eds Audrey Deacon and Peter Walne, Hertfordshire Record Publications 1987.
6 *Highways and Byways of Hertfordshire, op. cit.*

7 Richard Whitmore, *Hertfordshire Headlines,* Countryside Books 1987.

8 *Ibid.*

9 W. Branch Johnson, *Companion into Hertfordshire,* Methuen 1952.

10 Daniel Defoe, *A Tour Thro' the Whole Island of Great Britain,* first published 1724. Ed. G. D. H. Cole, Peter Davies 1927.

11 William Cobbett, *Rural Rides,* Ed. G. D. H. Cole, Peter Davies 1930.

12 *Victoria History of the Counties of England,* Vol. 1, 1902.

3 CONSUBURBATION

1 Sir William Beech Thomas, *Hertfordshire,* Robert Hale 1950.

2 Lionel M. Munby, *op. cit.*

3 *Bernard Shaw: Collected Letters 1898–1910,* ed. Dan H. Laurence, Max Reinhardt 1972.

4 Tony Rook, *A History of Hertfordshire,* Phillimore 1984.

5 *Encyclopaedia Britannica,* 1922 edn.

6 Lionel M. Munby, *op. cit.*

7 H. M. Alderman, *A Pilgrimage in Hertfordshire,* Trefoil 1931.

8 Arthur Mee, *Hertfordshire: London's Country Neighbour,* Hodder & Stoughton 1940.

9 H. M. Alderman, *op. cit.*

10 Reprinted in *Two Cheers for Democracy,* Edward Arnold 1951.

11 *Stevenage Herald,* 8 July 1988.

12 *Sunday Times,* 14 February 1988.

13 *The Times,* 30 January 1988.

4 ROMANS

1 'The Archaeology of Hertfordshire' in *Memorials of Old Hertfordshire,* ed. Percy Cross Standing, Bemrose 1905.

2 *A Professional Hertfordshire Tramp, op. cit.*

3 W. Branch Johnson, *Companion into Hertfordshire, op. cit.*

4 Sir William Beech Thomas, *op. cit.*

5 *Dictionary of National Biography.*

5 FOOTSTEPS

1 John Norden, *The Description of Hartfordshire*, 1597.
2 Ursula Buchan, *The Pleasures of Gardening*, Dent 1987.
3 *Hertfordshire & Bedfordshire Express*, 23 April 1949.
4 Ghost stories from *The Hertfordshire Village Book*, compiled by Hertfordshire Federation of Women's Institutes.

6 AUTHORS

1 William Hayley, *The Works of William Cowper, His Life and Letters, with Cowper's Private Correspondence*, ed. Revd T. S. Grimshawe, 1835.
2 Sir William Beech Thomas, *op. cit.*
3 J. A. Froude, *Carlyle*, 1882, 1884.
4 Quoted in Rudolph Robert, *Famous Authors in Hertfordshire*, Hertfordshire Countryside, n.d.
5 Tony Rook, *op. cit.*
6 See *Dictionary of National Biography*.
7 Michael Holroyd, 'Shaw at Shaw's Corner' in *Writers at Home*, ed. Gervase Jackson-Stops, Trefoil 1985.
8 James Lees-Milne, *Prophesying Peace*, Chatto & Windus 1977.
9 Ellen Terry, *The Story of My Life*, Hutchinson 1908.
10 *Over the Frontier*, Jonathan Cape 1938.

7 GODLINESS

1 *A Professional Hertfordshire Tramp*, *op. cit.*
2 Rudolph Robert, *op. cit.*
3 W. Branch Johnson, *Companion into Hertfordshire*, *op. cit.*
4 Wallace Notestein, *History of Witchcraft in England 1588–1718*, Oxford University Press 1911.

8 TOUR

1 *History Today*, October 1965.
2 Bodley Head 1971.

3 *The Marble Foot,* Collins 1976.
4 Herbert W. Tompkins, *op. cit.*
5 H. M. Alderman, *op. cit.*
6 *Memorials of Old Hertfordshire, op. cit.*
7 Quoted in Bernard Crick, *George Orwell: A Life,* Secker & Warburg 1980.
8 *The Diaries of Evelyn Waugh, op. cit.*

9 HOUSES

1 *In Search of English Gardens: The Travels of John Claudius Loudon and His Wife Jane,* ed. Priscilla Boniface, Lennard Publishing 1987.
2 W. Branch Johnson, *Companion into Hertfordshire, op. cit.*
3 *In Search of English Gardens, op. cit.*

10 WEN

1 Daniel Defoe, *op. cit.*
2 *Over the Frontier, op. cit.*
3 *Novel on Yellow Paper,* Jonathan Cape 1936.
4 W. Branch Johnson, *Companion into Hertfordshire, op. cit.*

INDEX

Abbot's Langley, 100
Adam, Robert, 117
Adrian iv, Pope (Nicholas Breakspear), 83
Akeman Street, 11, 22, 99
Alban, St, 44, 53
Albert, Prince Consort, 24
Albury, 109
Aldbury, 32, 81, 106, 143
Aldenham, 45, 138–9; reservoirs, 143; House, 122, 139; Manor (Bhaktivedanta Manor), 139
Aldenham, Henry Hucks (Vicary) Gibbs, 1st Baron, 50, 122, 139
Alderman, H. M.: *A Pilgrimage in Hertfordshire*, 58, 107
Alfred, King, 108
Alington, Elizabeth (*née* Tuffnell), 88
Alington, Revd John, 87–9
Allen, John, 93
Almshoe Bury (house), 130
animals, 104
Anne, Queen, 86
Anne Boleyn, Queen of Henry viii, 116
Anson, Admiral George, Baron, 117

Anstey, 102
Ant, Adam, 137
Arbuthnot, John, 106
Ardeley, 9, 113
Ash, river, 72, 109, 141
Ashridge Park (and house), 54, 81, 105, 107, 117, 119–20
Ashwell, 32, 42, 112–13, 142
Ashwell Bury, 125
Aspenden, 103
Aston Bury, 129
Austen, Jane, 76
Austin, Stephen, 146
Ayot St Lawrence, 20, 77–8

Bacon, Sir Francis, 51–3, 70
Bacon, Sir Nicholas, 24, 51–2, 117
Bailey, Frances, 93
Baldock, 12, 14, 15, 16, 19, 22, 28, 85, 90, 110–11, 146
Ball, John, 100
Balls Park, 130
Barkway, 24, 113
Barkway church, 87
Barley, 113

Barnet, 13, 75–6; Battles of, 136
barrows and burial mounds, 14–15
Bassus Green, 9
Bayford, 137, 138
Beane, river, 108, 113, 122, 129, 140, 141
Becket, St Thomas à, Archbishop of Canterbury, 35, 83, 103
Bedford, 2nd Countess of, 117
Bedmond, 83
Beeching Report, 1963 (on railways), 20
Being There (film), 56
Bengeo, 140
Benington, 32, 102, 120
Benington Lordship, 122
Beit family, 65, 122
Benskins Brewery, 139
Benslow Music Trust, 7
Berkhamsted, 11, 16, 67, 68, 83, 100, 101, 103–4, 106, 111, 143, 147; School, 104–5
Berners, Dame Juliana: *Book of St Albans* (attrib.), 48
Bessemer, Sir Henry, 141
Betjeman, John: 'Group Life, Letchworth', 29; 'Hertfordshire', 25, 26; 'The Town Clerk's View', 30, 36
Binham Priory, 4
Bishop's Stortford, 3, 39, 86, 109–10
Black Death, 33
Blakesware Manor, 72
Blondin, Charles, 17
Bluecoat School, Hertford, 139
Blythe, Ronald: *Divine Landscapes*, 3
Borehamwood, 144
Boudicca (Boadicea), Queen of the Iceni, 42–3
Bowen, Elizabeth, 66
Bowes-Lyon family, 122
Boxmoor, 145
Bourne, river, 109
Bragge, Revd Francis, 63, 86, 94–5
Bragge, Jane (*née* Chauncy), 86

Bramfield, 83
Braughing, 21, 32, 42, 65, 67, 113–14
brewing, 139–40
Bricket Wood, 38–9
Bride Hall, 130
Bridgewater family (Egertons), 119
Bridgewater, Francis Egerton, 3rd Duke of, 143
Brocket Hall, 117, 127, 136
Brocket, Charles Alexander Nall-Cain, 1st Baron, 42
Bromfield, William, 86
Brooke, Rupert, 127
Brookman's Park, 67, 83
Brown, Lancelot ('Capability'), 117
Brownlow, Edward John Peregrine Cust, 7th Baron, 104, 105
Broxbourne, 16, 86, 143, 149
Bryan, Lady, 117–18
Buchan, Ursula, 55
Bulbourne, river, 100, 141, 143, 144
Bulwer-Lytton, Edward, 1st Baron, 76, 136
Buntingford, 12, 33, 39, 87, 103, 111, 113
Bunyan, John, 24, 89
Burghley, Sir William Cecil, Baron, 51, 120
Bury (word), 130
Bushey, 11
Butt, Revd John Henry, 86
Butterfield, John, 95
Bygrave, 111
Byng, Admiral John, 136
Byron, George Gordon, 6th Baron, 127

Caesar, Julius, 41
Caldecote, 33–6
Caldecote, Thomas Inskip, 1st Viscount, 34
Caldecote, Robert Andrew Inskip, 2nd Viscount, 34
Calles, Helen, 92

Camfield Place, 80–1
canals, 142–3
Capel, Arthur, 1st Baron, 85
Caractacus, 42
Carlyle, Thomas, 71–2
Carmelites (friars), 6, 110
Cartland, Barbara, 36, 80
Cassiobury Park, 68, 128
Cassivellaunus, King of the
    Catuvellauni, 41–2, 128
Castle Acre priory, 4
Catherine of Aragon, Queen of Henry
    VIII, 116
Catherine Howard, Queen of Henry
    VIII, 116
Catholic Emancipation Act, 90
Catuvellauni (tribe), 41–2, 47
Chadwell, 142
chalk, 134
Champneys (health farm), 106–7
Chapman, George, 67
Chapmore End, 8
Charles I, King, 85, 123
Charles II, King, 59, 67, 85, 100, 126
Charlton, 8, 141
Charlton House, 141
Chartist Land Company, 32
Chaucer, Geoffrey, 104, 145
Chauncey, Arthur, 94
Chauncy, Charles, 55–6, 84
Chauncy, Sir Henry: on Boudicca, 43;
    on Sopwell Nunnery, 48; on Sir N.
    Bacon, 51; school and career, 56, 85;
    on spa waters, 75; and witchcraft,
    93–4, 96; on William I, 101; on
    Berkhamsted School, 105; on
    Ashridge, 119; on Knebworth, 125;
    and Hertford, 140; on river Rhee,
    142; *Antiquities of Hertfordshire*, 55–7,
    59
Chells, 45
Cherry-Garrard, Apsley, 108
Cherry Green, 12, 73

Cheshunt, 116, 133, 143
Chess, river, 141, 143
Chipperfield, 113
Chiswell Green, 121
Chorleywood, 32, 40, 139
Chiswell Green, 121
Chorleywood, 32, 40, 139
Christianity: arrival of, 43–4
churches: abandoned, 35; design, 83–4,
    131; history, 84–5
Churchill, Randolph, 2, 115
Civil War, English, 85
Clarendon, Henry Hyde, 2nd Earl of,
    138
class (social), 102–3
Claudius, Roman Emperor, 42
Clerke, William (of Chesfield), 85
Clinton family, 87
Clothall, 12, 28, 111
Clutterbuck, Robert, 62
coaching inns, 16–17
Cobbett, William, 13, 23, 55, 131, 133–
    5, 137, 144, 147
Cockburn, Claude, 105
Coleman Green, 89
Coleridge, Samuel Taylor, 71, 74, 139
Colley, Luke, 96–7
Colley, Wingfield, 66
Colne, river, 141, 143
Comet Hotel, Hatfield, 12
Common, Jack, 112
cottages, 130–1
Cottered, 12, 114
Cottered Lordship, 45
Cotton, Dr Nathaniel, 68
Country Gentlemen's Association, 29–
    30
Cow Roast, 106
Cowper, William, 1st Earl and Mary,
    Countess, 95, 123
Cowper, William (poet), 67–9
Crabb's Green, 11
Craig, Edward Gordon, 79

Croxley Green, 143
Cuffley, 75
Cunobelinus (Cymbeline), 42
Cussans, John Edwin, 17, 45, 57, 60, 62, 87
cycle clubs, 19

Datchworth, 65, 112
Day, Elizabeth, 93
Day, Fred, 20
Day, Ralph, 100
Defoe, Daniel, 14, 23, 89, 135
De Havilland aircraft factory, Hatfield, 27
De Havilland family, 65, 127
Delmé-Radcliffe family, 6, 91
Desborough, Ettie, Lady, 123, 135
deserted villages, 33–4
Dickens, Charles, 17, 76; *Bleak House*, 125
Dickinson, John, 145
Digswell, 17, 67
Dimsdale, Thomas, 109
Diocletian, Roman Emperor, 44
Dion Cassius, 43
Domesday Book, 33, 34, 101, 120
Donne, John, 69
Donovan (pop star), 137
Drage, William, 93
Duke o' York pub, 137
Dunstable, 22

Edmund of Langley, Duke of York, 100, 104
Edward I, King, 100
Edward III, King, 103
Edward VI, King, 117, 118–19
Edward, Black Prince, 103–4
Egerton family, 119
Eleanor of Castile, Queen of Edward I, 58
Elizabeth I, Queen, 24, 51, 100, 108, 117–20, 140

Elizabeth the Queen Mother, 42, 135
Ellis, William, 134
Elstree, 144–5
enclosure (of fields), 133
End: as name, 8–9
Ermine Street, 11, 39, 41, 124
Essendon, 80, 137
Essex, Robert Devereux, 2nd Earl of, 51
Essex, Arthur Capel, 1st Earl (of 7th creation), 60
Eustace of Boulogne, Count, 101
Evans, Dame Edith, 78
Exton, William, 5

Fairfax, Thomas, 3rd Baron, 85
Fanshawe family, 60
farming, 133–5
Ferrers, Kathleen, 65
Field, Mary, 72
fields, 22–3, 56, 111, 133–4
film-making, 144–5
Finchley, 13
Flamstead, 16, 56
Flaunden church, 87
flowers (wild), 24
Forster, E. M., 38; 'A Challenge for Our Time' (broadcast talk), 37; *Howards End*, 36
Fourdrinier, Henry, 145
Fox, George, 90
Fuller, Thomas: *The Worthies of England*, 55
Furbank, P. N., 36
Furneux Pelham Hall, 85

Gaddesden, Little and Great, 107
Gade, river, 100, 141, 143, 145
Gage, The (house), Little Berkhamsted, 137
game, 24–5
Garden Cities, 29–31, 33
Garden City Pioneer Company, 29

gardens and gardening, 54–5, 121–2, 128
Gardiner, Revd Godfrey, 93
Geary, Claude, 36
George I, King, 106
George VI, King, 42
Girton College, Cambridge, 57
Gobions, 83
Godwin, Edward William, 79
Golden Parsonage, 130
Goisbert de Beauvais, 101
Gore, William, 135
Gorhambury, 24, 46–7, 50–3, 117
Gosmore, 24, 141
Grand Junction Canal, 143, 145
Graveley, 3–4, 14, 24, 38, 84, 85
Great Amwell, 32, 70, 142
Great Nast Hyde, 130
Great North Road, 13–14
Great Wymondley, 42, 126
Green: as name, 8–9
Green Belt, 31, 38–9, 149
Green Dragon Hotel, Hertford, 20
Green, D., 146
Greene, Charles, 105
Greene, Graham, 105
Grim's Ditch, Berkhamsted, 101
Grimstone, Anna, 65
Grimthorpe, Edmund Beckett, 1st Baron, 49–50, 53, 122
Grove, The (house), Watford, 128
Groves, Manor of, 130
Gubblecote, 95–7
Guy, Henry, 135
Gwynn, Nell, 126
gypsies, 80

Hadley Wood, 136
Haileybury School, 57, 146
Hale family, 34
Hall, Mary, 93
Hall, Radclyffe, 136
Hammond, Barbara and J. J., 105–6

Hare Street, 12
Harkness (rose-growers), 40, 122
Harmsworth, Sir Alfred (*later* Viscount Northcliffe), 20
Harpenden, 45, 66, 79, 104, 136
Harrison, Johanna, 92
Harwood, Goodwife, 93
hat-making, 146–8
Hatfield, 15, 27, 40, 75, 146
Hatfield House, 66, 76, 118–21, 123, 137
Hatfield Tunnel, 12
Hawksmoor, Nicholas, 138
Hay Street, 12, 113
Hayley, William, 69
Hemel Hempstead, 11, 23, 27, 29, 40, 47, 134, 144, 148
Henderson (18th century comedian), 69
Henry II, King, 103
Henry VIII, King, 6, 49–50, 116, 118–19
Heronsgate, 32
Hertford, 15, 19, 20, 36, 54, 76, 90, 108–9, 137, 138, 140, 145
Hertfordshire Archaeological Review, 74–5
'Hertfordshire Hedgehogs', 41
Hertfordshire Mercury, 145
Hertfordshire Village Book, The, 97
Hexton, 111
High Cross, 21
Hilfield (*formerly* Sly's Castle), 138
Hilliard, Nicholas, 119
Hine, Reginald, 8, 33–4, 62–4, 87–8, 91
Hinxworth, 86
Hitchin, 2, 5–6, 16, 22, 40, 42, 62, 67, 78, 85, 86, 90–1, 110–11, 127, 140, 144, 147
Hitchin Priory, 6
Hiz, river, 141–2
Hoddesdon, 13, 16, 40, 59, 70, 111
Hoddesdon Park Wood, 41
Hook, Theodore, 74
Horse Cross, 65
house prices, 148–9

Howard, Ebenezer, 29–31
Hunsdon House, 117, 123
Hunsdon, Henry Carey, 1st Baron, 118
hunting parks, 120, 123
Hunton Bridge, 99
Huxley, Aldous, 81

Iceni (tribe), 43
Ickleford, 142
Ickleford Manor, 2, 115
Icknield Way, 22, 28, 33, 112, 113, 127, 142
industry, 144–7
Inskip, Wickham, 34
Irving, Sir Henry, 80
Ivel, river, 141

James I, King, 120–1, 123–4, 142
James II, King, 59, 86
James, Audrey, 115
Jekyll, Gertrude, 126
Jeoffrey de Magnaville, 101
John, King, 102
Johnson, Samuel, 91
Johnson, W. Branch, 21, 35, 59, 61, 91, 107
Jones, Inigo, 121
Jones, Revd William, 86
Julians (house), 114–15

Kayser-Bondor factory, Baldock, 28
Kelshall, 112
Ken, Thomas, Bishop of Bath and Wells, 67, 69
Kent, John, 129
Kimpton, 43
King, Mr (of Braughing), 114
King's Langley, 83, 100, 118
Knebworth, 14, 40
Knebworth House, 76, 118, 125
Knights Hospitallers, 111
Knights Templars, 15, 111, 126

Lafont, Revd Ogle Russell, 86
Lamb, Lady Caroline, 127

Lamb, Charles, 64, 70–3, 139
Lamb, Mary, 71
landscape, 22–3, 32–3
lanes, 18–19, 21–2
Langley, Edmund of, *see* Edmund of Langley, Duke of York
Laud, William, Archbishop of Canterbury, 55, 84
Lawes, Sir John Bennet, 134
Lea, river and valley, 40, 41, 59, 62, 70, 107–8, 127, 138, 140, 141–3, 146
Lees-Milne, James, 78
Lemsford, 127
leprosy, 111
Letchworth Garden City, 22, 29–30, 40, 146
Letchworth Hall, 88
Lévi-Strauss, Claude, 97
Lewis, Norman, 98
Lilly, 43
Lilly Hoo, 22, 127
Lincoln, John Thomas, Bishop of, 4
Little Berkhamsted, 67, 137
Local histories and historians, 55–8, 62–3
London: proximity of, 131–2, 133, 135
Long Marston, 95–7
Loudon, John Claudius and Jane, 121, 128
Lucas, Geoffrey, 7
Luton, 39, 146
Lutyens, Sir Edwin, 125
Lutyens, Lady Emily (*née* Lytton), 125–6
Lyde, Sir Lionel, 78
Lyth, Jisbella, 78
Lytton, Bulwer, *see* Bulwer-Lytton, Edward, 1st Baron
Lytton, Sir Robert, 125

McAdam, John Loudon, 16–17
Macaulay, Thomas Babington, Lord, 101–3

Mackery (Mackerye) End, 72–3
McMullens Brewery, 140
Magna Carta, 102
maltings, 140
Manor of Groves, *see* Groves, Manor of
Markyate, 16, 20, 68, 146
Markyate Cell, 65
Marlborough, Sarah, Duchess of (*née* Jennings), 128
Mary I (Tudor), Queen, 117–19
Maydencroft Manor, 141
Mee, Arthur, 34
Meetkerke, Adolphus, 114
Melbourne, William Lamb, 2nd Viscount, 127
Meux family, 124
Meux, Sir Henry, 124
Michael, King of Romania, 78
Mills, Joan, 93
Mimran, river, 17, 74, 108, 140, 141, 142
Minsden Chapel (St Nicholas's church, Minsden), 63–5
moats, 129
Monmouth, James Scott, Duke of, 116–17
Moor Park, *see* More, Manor of the
Moore, Henry, 109
Morden, Robert: *New Description and State of England*, 131
More, Manor of the (Moor Park), Rickmansworth, 116–17
More, Sir Thomas, 67, 83
motor cars, 19–21
motorways, 10, 99
Much Hadham, 57, 84, 109, 113, 134; Palace, 116
Munby, Lionel M.: *The Hertfordshire Landscape*, 33
Murchison, Sir Kenneth, 19
Myddelton, Sir Hugh, 142

Neville, George, Archbishop of York, 116

Newnham, 33, 34, 62
New River (canal), 59, 124, 142–3
New Towns, 27–30, 33
Newell, John and Joane, 92
Nicolson, (Sir) Harold, 66
Norden, John, 23, 54
Norman Conquest, 101–2
Northaw, 133
Northchurch, 106
North Mimms, 134
nudist colonies, 39

O'Connor, Feargus, 32
Odo, Bishop of Bayeux, 101
Offa, King of Mercia, 44, 49
Offley, 43
Offley church, 87
Oman, Carola, 85
ordeal, trial by, 94–6
Orwell, George and Eileen, 111–12
Osborn, Ruth and John, 95–7
Oughton, river, 141–2

Palmerston, Henry John Temple, 3rd Viscount, 127
Panshanger estate, 30, 67, 123
paper-making, 145
Park Street, 47
parks, 135
Paternoster, Ellen, 7
Paul family, 77, 122
Peet, Samuel, 90
Pepys, Samuel, 13, 27, 74–5, 90, 146
Perry Green, 109
Peter de Valognes, 101
Peter the Wild Boy, 106
Pevsner, Sir Nikolaus: *Hertfordshire*, 29, 33, 50, 104, 128, 134, 138
Pickford, Thomas, 16
Pile, Stephen, 38
Pirton, 102, 111
Pishiobury, 130
Pitman, Dr (schoolmaster), 68
place names, 8, 130

plaiting (straw), 146–8
Plumer, Colonel John, 95
population numbers, 26–7
Porters Park, 138
Poston, Elizabeth, 36–8
Potter, Beatrix, 80
Potters Bar, 19, 40, 45, 83, 136–7
Potters Green, 21
Powell, J. Enoch, 100
Powell, Justice, 95
Poynders End (farm), 5, 7–8, 63
Poyntz-Stewart family, 4
Prescott, Sir George, 59
Preston, 5, 21, 24, 43, 89, 126
Preston, Revd Matthew Morris, 103
printing, 145–6
Prout family, 134
Puckeridge, 13, 21, 113
Purwell, river, 43

Quakers, 5–6, 89–91
Queen Hoo, 130
Quennell, Peter, 105–6
Quin, river, 67, 113, 114, 141
Quinbury, 67

Radcliffe family, 6
Radlett, 47, 138
Radwell, 34–5
railways, 17–18, 20–1
Raleigh, Sir Walter, 51, 123
Ralph de Limesie, 101
Ravensburgh Castle, 111
Reade, Charles, 79
Redbourn, 16, 23, 33, 46
Red Hills track, 41
Reed, 24, 112, 128–9
Repton, Humphry, 67
Rhee, river, 141, 142
Rhodes, Cecil, 109–10
rhododendron, 54–5
Rib, river, 21, 35, 103, 141
Richard II, King, 100, 104

Rickmansworth, 40, 143, 149
Ridge, 138
rivers, 141–2
Robert de Mortain, 101
Robinson, Lieutenant William Leefe,
    VC, 137
Romans: roads, 11–12; subjugate
    Britain, 41–3; towns and remains, 42–
    3, 45–7; settlements, 44
Rook, Tony, 74–5
Rook's Nest, Stevenage (house; model
    for Howards End), 36–8
roses, 121–2
Rothamsted, 134
Rothschild, Baron Lionel Nathan de, 107
Rothschild, Walter, 2nd Baron, 107
Royal National Rose Society, 121
Royston, 3, 13, 22, 39, 136–7; cave, 14–
    15; origins, 33; James I's House, 123–
    4; Cobbett on, 137
Royston Club, 89
Royston Heath, 16, 123
Rumbold, Richard, 60
Rushden, 86, 112, 114
Rye House, 56–92

Sackville-West, Vita, 66
Sacombe, 17
St Albans, 16, 33, 40, 83, 92, 101, 111,
    120, 146, 148; medieval pilgrimages
    to, 12; abbey (cathedral), 44–5, 48–50,
    110; description and history, 46–9;
    see also Verulamium
St Albans, Charles Beauclerk, 1st Duke
    of, 126
St Etheldreda (church), Chesfield, 4
St Ippollitts, 141
St Paul's Walden, 21, 58
St Paul's Walden Bury, 122
Salisbury, Robert Cecil, 1st Earl of, 121,
    123
Salisbury, Cecily Alice Cecil,
    Marchioness of, 135

Salisbury, Marjorie Cecil, Marchioness of, 121
Salisbury, Mary Amelia Cecil, Marchioness of, 76
Salisbury Hall, 126–7
Salmon, Nathaniel, 57, 62
Sandon, 9, 112
Sandridge, 128
Sarratt, 100
Sawbridgeworth, 3, 109, 134
Saxton, Christopher, 11
Scott, Sir George Gilbert, 50
Scott, John (of Amwell), 91, 142
Scott, Sir Walter, 130
Seebohm, Benjamin, 5
Seebohm, Derrick, 5, 8
Seebohm, Esther (*née* Wheeler), 5
Seebohm, Esther, 7
Seebohm, Fidelity, 5
Seebohm, Freda, 7
Seebohm, Frederic, 5–7, 91
Seebohm, Frederic (Lord Seebohm of Hertford), 8
Seebohm, George, 4–5
Seebohm, Hilda, 7
Seebohm, Hugh, 5, 7, 91
Seebohm, Juliet, 7
Seebohm, Mary Ann (*née* Exton), 5
Seebohm, Winnie, 7
Sellers, Peter, 56
Seymour of Sudeley, Thomas, Baron, 119
Shakespeare, William: *Henry VI, pt 2*, 136; *Richard II*, 100
Shaw, George Bernard, 20, 77–80; *John Bull's Other Island*, 31
Shell Guide to Hertfordshire, 34
Shenley, 21, 138
Shephall, 27
Shorthale, Robert, 3
Simmonds, James, 59
Simmons, Ann, 72
Six Hills, 14

Skingle, Daniel, 63
Smith, John (of Graveley), 3
Smith, Stevie, 81–2, 136, 138
soil, 54, 56
Sootfield Green, 8
Sopwell Nunnery, St Albans, 48
South, Mary Anne, 77
South Mimms, 126
Southey, Robert, 71
spa waters, 75
stagecoaches, 16
Standon, 86, 118
Stane Street, 42
Stansted, 39
Stevenage, 10, 14, 16, 17, 19, 27–30, 35, 37–8, 40, 45, 76–7, 79, 129
Stocking Pelham, 10–11
Stort, river, 59, 109, 141
Strathmore, Cecilia Nina, Countess of, 135
Stretton, Jane, 92
Strutt, Revd Robert, 94
Strutt, Joseph: *Queenhoo-Hall*, 130
Styles, Benjamin Hoskyns, 117
Suetonius (Roman governor), 43
supermarkets, 28
surnames, 8
Swift, Jonathan, 117

Tankerfield, George, 50
Tasciovanus, 42
Tate, John, 145
Tawney, R. H., 105
Telegraph Hill, 22
Telford, Thomas, 15
Temple, Sir William, 117
Temple Bar, 124–5
Temple Dinsley, 126
Terry, Ellen, 79–80
Tewin, 24, 65, 118
Tewin Water, 122, 127
Theobalds Park, 59, 120, 123–4, 142
Therfield, 102, 112

Thomas, Sir William Beech, 63, 126; *Hertfordshire*, 58–9, 61
Thompson, Emma, 149
Thundridge, 35
tollgates, 13–14, 17
Tompkins, Herbert W., 14, 18–19, 57, 62, 73, 90, 107, 114, 148; *Highways and Byways of Hertfordshire*, 19
Tradescant, John, the elder, 121
Trevelyan, George Macaulay, 106
Tring, 3, 11, 22, 97, 105–7, 127, 135, 143, 147
Trinovantes (people), 42
Trollope, Anthony, 77
Trollope, Thomas, 114
Troubridge, Una, Lady, 136
turnpikes, 13–14, 17
Tyttenhanger (house), 130

Unwin, Mary, 68–9

Ver, river, 141
Verulam House, 52–3
Verulamium, 33, 42–5, 47; theatre, 46–7; *see also* St Albans
Vespasian, Roman Emperor, 42
Victoria County History (Hertfordshire), 57
Victoria House, Gosmore, 141

Wadesmill, 14, 16
Walkern, 9, 93–4, 102, 113
walkers and walking, 18–19
Wallington, 18, 19, 111–12, 113
Waltham Cross, 58–9, 70, 77, 122, 143
Walton, Ann, 69
Walton, Izaak, 60, 69–70
Ward, Mrs Humphry, 81, 106
Ware, 13, 14, 35, 39, 70, 91, 108, 120, 137, 139, 140; Great Bed of, 60
Wareside, 72
Water End, 127–8
Watford, 11, 40, 62, 128, 133, 140, 143, 146
Watling Street, 11, 22, 46
Watson, Mary Spencer, 4

Watton House, 129
Watton at Stone, 17, 21, 65
Watts, George Frederic, 79
Waugh, Auberon, 2
Waugh, Evelyn, 2, 115
Wells, Frank, 67
Wells, H. G., 10, 67
Welwyn (Old), 14, 16, 19, 42, 46, 74–5
Welwyn Archaeological Society, 75
Welwyn Garden City, 27, 30–1, 40, 42, 102, 123, 144, 149
Welwyn Viaduct, 17
Wenham, Jane, 93–5
Wesley, John, 15, 90
West, Anthony, 67
West, Dame Rebecca, 67
Westmill, 32, 62, 73, 113
Weston, 24, 38, 111, 146
Whempstead, 21
Wheathampstead, 42, 89, 107–8
Whitbread, Samuel, 80
White, Joan, 92
Whitwell, 43, 142
Widford, 72
Wigginton, 101, 106–7, 135
William I (the Conqueror), King, 101, 108–10, 120
Willian, 63
Wilstone, 97
Wine Society, The, 30
witches and witchcraft, 92–7
Wolsey, Thomas, Cardinal, 116, 126
Woodhall Park, 127
Woodhouse, Dr Christopher, 93
Wordsworth, William, 71
Wormleybury, 127
Wren, Sir Christopher, 124
Wrotham Park, 117, 136

York, Duke of, *see* Edmund of Langley, Duke of York
Young, Arthur, 134, 147
Young, Edward, 73–5